A PICTURESQUE TALE OF PROGRESS

By Olive Beaupré Miller

Assisted by Harry Neal Baum

BEGINNINGS

PART I

THE BOOK HOUSE FOR CHILDREN

CHICAGO

PRINTED IN U.S.A.

FOREWORD

By OLIVE BEAUPRÉ MILLER

NO STORY that could be written is more thrilling, more dramatic, in its colorful episodes, than the actual story of history, the story of mankind's struggle for progress through all the ages past. Yet I myself emerged from high school and college with only a dry collection of dates, a jumbled memory of many apparently meaningless wars, and a fragmentary, disconnected knowledge of a very few periods in history, through which I could follow no continuous thread of the actual forward march of man. Moreover, history had never been presented to me as though it concerned human beings whose lives were more full of human interest, of tragedy, comedy, romance and great adventure than those of the hero in any novel. So I left college determined not only to get for myself a connected and general view of history, but to make that history alive in my own imagination. For years I pursued this work as a hobby, writing it up in notebooks for my own satisfaction and pleasure. And as I gradually acquired an over-all picture of history, I began to see a thread running through all its incidents. I began to see the story of man's slow struggle upward from the mere mastery of his environment, through ever increasing use of the powers of his mind and ever increasing release for his creative abilities, to the dawning within him of a ceaseless search for a better social order and better forms of government.

Then at last came my opportunity to give children what I myself had wanted from childhood on—a picturesque and living history of the world from the Stone Age to the beginnings of modern times. So I delved enthusiastically into further research and visited or revisited many foreign countries. In Egypt, Palestine, Syria, Greece, Crete, Italy and all the other countries of Western Europe, in Mexico, with its glorious remains of Aztec culture, in Yucatan, where lie the ruins of the splendid Maya cities, I traveled highways and byways in search of atmosphere and knowledge. And wherever I went I combed museums collecting pictures of their archaeological exhibits that I might make accurate the backgrounds against which the drama of history was enacted. To bring history to life for children, to present to them a fascinating historical panorama, to let them travel up the path of time with the men and women who had made history—that was my purpose in writing A PICTURESQUE TALE OF PROGRESS.

I saw no reason at all why tales of the lives of great people and of the most thrilling events should not have all the vivid dramatic action that is in a story book and still be kept absolutely authentic, absolutely in line with facts. And I had working with me, as a most able assistant, Mr. Harry Neal Baum, who had been an instructor in history at the University of Wisconsin. Between us we mapped out the scope of the books and gathered the material. Then I wrote it up in its final form and we checked and rechecked the finished manuscript for accuracy in all details.

My plan was not only to present a text that would interest children, but to impress upon them the facts contained in that text by telling the story all over again in the illustrations and the notes beneath them. I aimed also to give the child by means of these illustrations some knowledge of the art, the architecture, the manner of life, the customs and costumes of the various peoples with whom I dealt. So Mr. Baum and I assembled and have reproduced in these books an amazing number of pictures from original sources— from archaeological discoveries, collections of artifacts in museums, and paintings and carvings of the past, wherein men have depicted the life of their own times as they themselves saw it. And whenever we employed an artist to make an imaginative picture of a certain period, we required him to use the source material with which we furnished him, so that all costumes, all pottery, all furniture or whatever else appeared in his drawing should be, not the result of his own fancy only, but of the authentic models which had been given him. Thus in addition to making the story still more alive the pictures were designed to answer the question children so often ask, "How do you know people lived like that at that time?" by showing them the source material from which our knowledge comes.

It is true that children must be at least ten years old before they are ready for any *consecutive* story of history. The very small child has no sense of past time at all. To him Moses and his own mother and father lived in the very same era. But gradually when he is around six the child does get the idea that people once lived differently from the way he is living now. Then he begins to be greatly interested in how prehistoric men lived, though he is still apt to startle his father or mother, if one of them is reading to him about the cave men, by looking up and asserting, "And you were living then, too!" Nevertheless, it is at this moment that we have first tried to get the child's interest and we have done so by inventing some imaginary characters in telling the story of prehistoric man, that children of six or seven, as well as the older children, might truly enjoy it. But as soon as we come to Egypt

and the earliest actually recorded history, we have dropped imaginary characters save in a very few instances, telling the story as it really was, directing it
toward children old enough to grasp its meaning and to adults, for their enjoy-
ment as well.

Mainly, we have followed one line of culture which came directly from
the dawn of history to us today. So after the section on prehistoric man, we
begin with Egypt because our civilization in the United States came straight
down to us through ever accumulating knowledge from Egypt. Trading, as
the Egyptians did, across the Mediterranean, they carried what they knew
to that island of sea-kings, Crete, taking back to Egypt what had been
learned by the very progressive people of Crete. And this accumulation of
information, Crete passed on to Greece. Then, with the store of knowledge
ever increasing, Greece passed it on to Rome, whence it spread to Western
Europe—to Spain, Italy, Britain, France, Germany and the Netherlands.
And from the peoples of these European countries, who settled in America,
the line was passed on to us. Egypt, Crete, Greece, Rome, Western Europe,
the United States—that is the line which ties up the oldest ancient history
with us and our children today.

But in going along with our story Mr. Baum and I have gathered into this
main stream of culture numerous tributary streams which added something
to it. Then we have told the background stories of all the great nations of
Europe and Asia, including China, Japan and India. And in the eighth volume
we have given the background of the last peoples to enter the stream of world
history, our neighbors in Mexico, Central and South America, who glory in
their descent from great American Indian tribes. Thus we have rounded out
and completed our purpose in writing these books, which was to introduce
the child to all the important nations of the world and to present to him, as
a foundation for the study of modern history, the various backgrounds which
have made these nations so different from each other in temperament, in
traditions and ideologies. Always we have tried to point out the contribution
to history made by each race and each great individual. We have also tried
to show in each period what were the permanent elements of growth and
what were the elements of destruction, thereby making clear those lessons of
experience which the past can teach the present. And the summaries at the
end of each volume form, if read consecutively, an interesting picture of the
whole sweep of history during the period we have covered, with the meaning
of events conveyed plainly and *the significance they have for us brought down to
the world of today.*

The ninth volume consists of an index by means of which any special subject may be pursued. With the help of this index, not only parents and teachers, but the child himself can trace a single thread of progress from its beginning. He can find out about the evolution of language, of writing, of literature, of transportation, of religion, of business. He can trace the development of art from the first crude drawings of cave men to the exquisite paintings of the great Italian masters of the Renaissance. He can trace the evolution of government from the first simple rule of a chieftain over his tribe to the rule of kings and emperors, and the time when the Romans established a republic. Then through the long years of keeping the masses in bondage, he can see more and more groups and kinds of people beginning to demand some representation in the government through such bodies as the English Parliament.

So in every way possible I have tried to make these books not only accurate and interesting, but usable to a child. And why was I so eager to interest children in history? Why should you and I and all of us want our children to know the great stories of history? Because we would have them learn from both the successes and the failures of men and movements in the past what they will need to know as adults to form intelligent opinions about the problems of the present and the future. Because we would have them know the past of those nations of the world with whom we have at last come into such close contact, in order that they may understand what these people are, why they think, feel and act as they do. And because, through all the centuries of struggle and experience which lie behind our heritage of today, we would have our children catch a glimpse of the goal toward which history tends— more and more freedom for more and more people, more and more opportunity for the fulfillment of all man's innate capacities.

CONTENTS

LIST OF MAPS

THE PICTURE ON THE COVER *is taken from a wall-painting in the rock tomb of Ahmes at El Amarna. It represents Pharaoh Akhnaton of Egypt and his wife, Queen Nefertiti, with one of their little girls, just as they are leaving Akhnaton's wonderful palace in his new "City of the Horizon of Aton." The chariot is gaily decorated and the prancing steeds are gorgeous in their feathered headdress. A touch of naturalness appears in the attempt of the little princess to poke the horses with a stick.*

I

How People Lived a Long Time Ago

Early Stone Age

(ABOUT 150,000 B.C. TO 50,000 B.C.)

At the edge of the great forest grows the tall jungle grass. The wind is playing over it, stirring silver-green waves in the sun. Bird calls and monkey chatter shrill from the vine-hung treetops. Cautiously some living thing is winding through the grass. Now the ripple of shimmering blades closes over its head; now the long grass parts, and there appears a figure, squat, bow-legged and burly, with matted hair in a mass hanging to the shoulders. The face is almost chinless; the nose is broad and flat; the little eyes, beneath bulging brows, are peering everywhere, seeking, always seeking.

That is Father the Hunter, Father the Protector, bearing

a stone in one hand and a heavy club in the other. Behind him follows the family. All are alert and watchful; eyes and ears are open. They must catch the smallest hint of any approach of danger—cave bears or a sabre-tooth tiger may lurk near in the jungle. They are all of them searching for food, for berries, herbs or nuts, or perhaps for some bird or small beast which Father may bring down with the stone or club in his hand. And when they catch a wild pig, what grunts of satisfaction! How greedily they tear it, rip it up with their fingers, and noisily eat it raw!

It was a long time ago that Father and the family went hunting for food in this manner. Men were wilder in those days than the wildest savage today. They had no homes to live in; they had no fire to cook with; they did not even wear clothing. But it was very warm where they lived. The sun shone brightly all day long; the earth was covered with giant trees, a wild and pathless jungle, where family groups wandered about, eating wild fruits and nuts, hunting small game, and drinking from rivers and streams.

"Tiger!"

One sharp cry from Father, and quicker than thinking they run! They leap, they scramble, they spring up the limbs

The skull of the "dawn man," the earliest man known to have lived upon earth, was found in Piltdown, Sussex, England, in 1911-12. Together with the skull in the shallow pit of dark-brown gravel where it was discovered, there was a small piece of flint which had been chipped and shaped for use. This man is thought to have lived more than 100,000 years ago. He is sometimes called the Piltdown man, from the place where he was found.

of the nearest tree. Even Mother, with Baby clutched safe in one arm, climbs to the topmost branches.

The dreaded roar of the man-eater terrifies the whole forest. The birds and the monkeys are quiet, cowering in the treetops. Creeping with quiet feet, the sabre-tooth shows himself, gleaming among the grasses; but this time his prey has escaped him. They are high up out of his reach, hidden away in the treetops. Snarling and lashing his tail, he tramples the ground for hours, waiting below to catch them. But the family will not come down. If need be, they will sleep in the tree. The tiger must slink away and seek some prey less agile.

Most of the time, however, the family stays on the ground. When night comes they find a hollow, fill it well with leaves, and all cuddle down together, huddled in a heap, in order to keep themselves warm and protect each other from danger. And so they sleep wherever they are, until the bright sunshine awakes them to begin another day.

Father has very few words. He can scarcely talk with Mother. He can only utter rude noises like the sounds that are made by things. "Swish" means a stone or a stick; for sticks make a swishing sound as they are thrown through the air. A rumbling growl means a bear; a sharp "Yip-Yip" means a fox; a bird-call means a bird. And to tell any fact about objects Father has to make signs, or help out his grunts with acting.

Father runs up to Mother, a warning light in his eyes. "Gr-rr!" he growls. He means "bear," and he points away to the forest. A bear is in the forest. Can he be coming their way? Shall Mother flee to the treetops? No; Father lies down and closes his eyes. The bear is asleep or dead—if dead, then Father will take them all to eat the beast in the forest. But Father springs up and leads them off in the other direction entirely. The bear is asleep in the forest. Mother understands. They must take good care not to rouse him.

In just such a manner as this, thinking little, but ever alert to any sign of danger, active in body, but sluggish in mind, men had lived on the earth for 200,000 years, wandering up and down, crossing into Europe from Asia, whence all races seemed to spring, and tramping wherever they chose.

How the Cold Changed the Family's Life
(About 50,000 B.C.)

Now no one thought much of the weather until the cold grew so intense that the family, which lived in those days, began to suffer severely. The sun was hidden from sight a great part of the day, and cold rains came with sleet and driving storms of snow. Herds of reindeer came southward with the mammoth and woolly rhinoceros. The mammoth looked like an elephant except that he had shaggy hair and grew to be twelve feet tall. With his head held high in the air, this great beast tramped the earth, brandishing threatening tusks from eight to ten feet long. But the mammoth and woolly rhinoceros were both grass-eating creatures, which rarely fell upon man unless they were roused to anger. It was the huge cave lion, cave bear, cave leopard, and sabretooth tiger, from which men had to flee; for these were man-eating beasts, too large to be attacked when men had no stouter weapons than a sharp stone or a club.

This is one of the very earliest paintings upon the walls of a cave. It was cut in the rock about 25,000 B.C., and shows how the mammoth looked to the people living in those days. This animal was quite like the elephant in build, but was covered with long shaggy, reddish hair, and had a curious, dome-shaped head, with immensely long tusks of ivory on either side of the trunk. There are no mammoths living upon earth today, and they are known only by their bones and the pictures which the earliest people drew on the walls of their caves.

The woolly rhinoceros is another animal not found on earth today. It was a clumsy creature with one cruel-looking horn growing upright on its snout and a shorter one on its forehead, and with a thick shaggy coat as a protection from the cold. This picture was painted by early man in the cavern of Font-de-gaume, France, about 18,000 B.C. The outline is in red ochre with shading and a few lines to represent the hairy coat.

The snow on the mountains grew thicker, and heavy ice covered the rivers. Gradually all the snow turned to ice, taking the form of glaciers and slipping down the mountain sides into the nearby valleys.

Although the family never dreamed of such a remarkable fact, this was the fourth time that snow and ice had covered much of the world; and each time that those great glaciers had swept away to the southward, all living things had died, and trees and plants had been frozen or pressed down into the bogs, to be found ages later as coal.

The earth itself had changed. Mountains had been heaved up, others had been worn down by the grind of the rivers of ice. Lakes had formed and vanished. Land had appeared and disappeared, now connecting continents, now leaving them isolated, surrounded by wastes of sea.

But in days of warmth and fertile growth, between those long times of freezing, gigantic beasts had walked the earth, like beasts in some strange dream. Sometimes, the family, wandering about, came on remains of these animals, giant petrified eggs or skeletons in the rock, left there thousands

The family have found the skeleton of a pter'o-dac'tyl. This was a flying reptile which had lived many thousands of years before, in one of the warm times between glacial periods. The pterodactyl had a long beak, a very small body and enormous wings measuring more than twenty feet from tip to tip when outspread. The artist has drawn this picture from a skeleton found in the rocks of Bavaria, Germany. Other skeletons have been found in the United States and Brazil. All these queer animals disappeared from earth before the age of man.

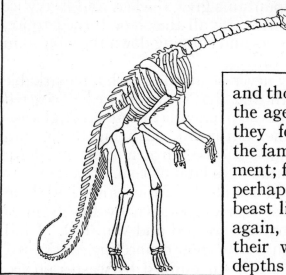

This is the skeleton of a very large di'no-saur found in Arizona but now in the American Museum of Natural History, New York. The dinosaur was the largest land animal that ever lived; this one was sixty-five feet long and weighed nearly forty tons. The tail alone was over twenty feet in length and this helped balance the great beast when it stood upon its hind legs, as it undoubtedly did most of the time. The front legs were much shorter and weaker than the hind legs and probably were of very little use to the animal in getting around on the ground or in fighting its enemies.

and thousands of years before the age of man. And when they found these remains, the family hissed with excitement; for they thought that perhaps, sometime, a strange beast like this might appear again, looming up to bar their way in the shadowy depths of the forest.

They found the bones of di'no-saurs, immense and fantastic creatures, measuring eighty-four feet from their heads to the tips of their

tails and having long snake-
like necks, with which they
reached up to eat leaves from
the tops of the tallest trees,
rising on their hind legs like
enormous kangaroos. They
came now and then on skeletons embedded in the rock—
the ugly tri-cer'a-tops, like a
great horned hippopotamus;
sea-lizards, thirty feet long;
and the waddling pa'lae-o-scin-
cus, a giant hard-shelled tur-
tle, with sharp, horn-covered
spines. But the family's fear

In spite of their great size, some of the dinosaurs did
not like the taste of meat, but fed only upon vegetable
foods and used their long necks to reach the tenderest
leaves upon the treetops. Balanced upon tail and
hindlegs, they would hold the branches in their short
forelegs, as they nibbled at choice bits of foliage.

of meeting these beasts was quite without foundation; for
they had vanished long ago, before there were men on the
earth, buried in the engulfing clutch of on-coming rivers of ice.

Here are the tri-cer'a-tops and the pa'lae-o-scin'cus as they appeared in the swampy country when the earth was
very warm. The artist has drawn this picture from skeletons of these animals found in the rocks of Arizona and Montana.

Clothing and the First Tool

The family suffered so much from the cold, that Father was quite unable to keep them warm with leaves; but one day the smallest Man-child, creeping under the hide of a bear which his Father had cast aside when he skinned the beast for supper, found that a bear-skin gave warmth. "Bear-skin warm," he grunted.

Father had noticed what Man-child had done, and for the first time he began to think, to work out a simple plan. After breakfast, he chopped at the skin until he had cut it in pieces. Then he fastened these pieces on the bodies of each of his children, over the left shoulder, and under the right arm, leaving the right arm free. The children were delighted! For the first time they were warm! For the first time they had clothing. For the first time man had used his wits to conquer his difficulties! And ever afterwards people wore clothing of some kind.

The next day Father sat under a tree tossing into the air the sharp stone he had used when he cut the bear-skin.

"Ugh, ugh!" grunted Father, by which he meant to say: "Small stone too much work! Need big hack-hack stone!"

But the larger stones were smooth and round, and had no sharp edge to cut with; so Father grunted again, and this time he meant to say: "Hunter-man make edge! Hunter-man make edge on big, big hack-hack stone!"

Searching all about, he chose a large, gray rock. Then he made a work-bench by placing a large flat stone on the ground before the tree. Holding the hard, gray rock braced against his bench, he took his small sharp stone, and struck the rock a blow.

Crack, crack, crack! For a time nothing happened at all, and then all at once a chip broke away from the rock, a layer that tapered off, leaving a thin, sharp edge.

"Hi, yi!" yipped Father, pleased.

Hour after hour, he crouched there, striking away at the rock, while Man-Child crept up and watched him, eager and breathless with interest.

Crack, crack, crack! All day long, crack, crack!

As long as the daylight lingered, Father continued his work. So many blows had to be struck before a piece broke

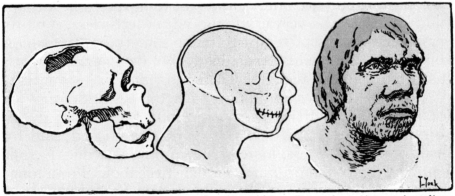

Certain men who have made a life study of the skulls and bones of the earliest people are able to put pieces of bone together and to build up "flesh" on these bones so that they can show almost exactly how these people looked when they lived upon the earth so many thousands of years ago.

The skull at the left is all that has been found of the head of a Ne-an'der-thal man who lived between 50,000 B.C. and 25,000 B.C. near La Chapelle-aux-Saints in central France.

The skull was not found as the picture shows it, but in many different pieces which had to be put together very carefully. Then from holes in the jaw bones and from the bones about the mouth it was possible to place in a plaster cast of the skull, the proper size teeth and the right kind of nose. When these parts had been added, plaster eyeballs were placed in the eye-sockets, and the flesh part of the head added. This is shown in orange in the center drawing. The flesh was molded very carefully to follow the bone part of the skull, and a great deal of special knowledge and skill was necessary in shaping the flesh over the forehead, around the nose and mouth and about the chin.

The last picture on the right shows the plaster model with the outer skin and hair added, and this is how the Neanderthal man looked. The model is not that of any one man, but is representative of the whole race.

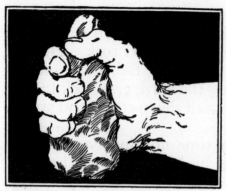

One end of the fist hatchet was made smaller than the other and was rounded and smoothed so that it could be grasped firmly without hurting the hand. The other end was bigger and just as sharp as it could be made, so that the cuts would be long and deep.

off, and, as Father worked toward an edge, he had to be much more careful. He had to give lighter taps and break off smaller pieces. It was not an easy task. Not until noon of the second day had the rock been given an edge, circular, like a chopping knife, and about three inches long.

"Hi, yi!" yipped Father in triumph as he gripped the stone in his fist.

"Hi, yi!" echoed Smallest Man-Child, thrilled with intense excitement. And he seized the hatchet himself and split a piece of bone.

So Father's hack-hack stone became the first fist-hatchet. Of course, it had no handle, and had to be used like a chopping knife. It was very crude indeed; nevertheless, it represented man's first attempt to make something, to fashion something to meet his needs, instead of being content with just what he could pick up. Here was man's first invention.

Afterward, Father found flint to be the best kind of stone for hatchets. Flint is very hard, but is made of many thin layers, between which a stone can be pushed; and by prying off these layers, instead of chipping his edge, Father found he could make a much more perfect tool. For a long, long time, however, no other shape was thought of, and the fist hatchet remained the only tool and weapon of man.

The First Home

In their new skin clothing the family were happier and far more comfortable than they had been before, but how very cold the wind was! Day after day the snow fell, and the ice crept nearer and nearer their sheltered little valley. A cave would be warm and comfortable, but Father feared those dark holes; bears, hyenas, leopards, and other wild beasts lived in them. One day, however, he found himself weary and nearly frozen after a day of hunting. A cave yawned darkly before him. If only he dared to enter it! But he could not muster his courage. The shadows were deep and mysterious. The walls seemed to close upon him.

And then a sound startled him suddenly—the snort of a maddened animal, enraged by some unknown fear! In a moment he saw coming toward him over a nearby hill-top an enormous, woolly rhinoceros, plunging, snorting, fierce!

There was no time for thinking. Swiftly Father sprang forward. Before he knew it, he was in the cave, crouching, trembling, hiding. The great beast came heavily on; but he himself was fleeing. Some danger threatened him, too. Panting and terrified, he passed the mouth of the cave and disappeared in the distance.

And now Father dared to breathe and slowly looked about him. How warm it was in that shelter—no snow and no biting winds. And the place was free of wild beasts. It was cozy! It was comfortable! The floor was covered with bits of rock. The ceiling was higher than a man could reach and far overhead a bit of light filtered in through small cracks, partly dispelling the darkness, and keeping the air fresh and pure. Here was a home for his family. Here were safety and shelter. He grunted with satisfaction and hurried off to his mate. She must come with the children and see how cozy and warm it was in the depths of that long, dark cave.

The family filed in after Father, curiously peering about. Ah, it was good to be out of the wind! A cave was the place for a home! A cave was a real shelter! They had no fire it is true, and their beds were only dry leaves, but in all their lives before, they had never been so protected.

This cave is drawn from a photograph of the entrance to the cavern of La Chapelle-aux-Saints, France, where the most perfectly preserved skeletons of the Neanderthal men were found.

The First Fire

The longer Father and the family lived in their cave, the more they liked it. The family had grown in size with the passing years, and there were now a number of boys and girls of different ages to help in hunting and gathering food.

The cave gave them a place where they could keep the nuts, herbs, and berries which they gathered, and the boys often helped Father find stones and chip them into hatchets. The pile of animal skins grew until there were more than enough for clothes and covering, and some were used to make bags for carrying and storing.

It continued to snow most of the time, and when summer came, it was not the warm summer Father remembered years ago, but more like autumn. The winds were sharp and biting always; the trees put out leaves for a few months only. Even the sun did not seem to shine as warmly as it had before. When Father went toward the mountains in his search for food, he came upon great thick sheets of ice where no animals lived, and the land was utterly bare.

Still, the family was happy and fairly comfortable. The

skin robes protected their bodies and the cave gave both
warmth and shelter.   Other families passed them occasionally, journeying toward the south where they hoped to find
warmer sunshine.   But Father and the family liked their
cave home so much that they remained where they were.

And then one night a terrific storm went raging through
the valley.   The snow turned to wet, biting sleet and back
again to snow.   Great black clouds darkened the sky, and
rolled and thundered overhead.   Occasionally, a flash of
lightning illuminated the heavens.

It was much too disagreeable for any of the family to venture to go out.   Through the long afternoon, they sat, huddled in the cave, uneasy and afraid. At night, they dozed off to
sleep, but often they awoke, startled by some strange sound.

Toward morning, there came a crash that brought them
all to their feet.   The plain in front of the cave was lighted
by a glare, lurid, weird, fantastic, coming and going fitfully
and throwing unearthly shadows far into the depths of the
cave.   Soon the strong acrid smell of burning filled the air.
This was a new experience, and, as always with something

new, the family was afraid.   They lay in trembling quiet till the storm had passed them by.

Then Father ventured to leave the cave and see what had occurred.   The lightning had struck a dead tree standing at the edge of the forest, and the tree was all ablaze.   The flames died down and rose again; heavy smoke mounted the sky, and bits of burning twigs now and then fell to the ground.

Cautiously, the family came out to see this strange new sight; and as they drew near the tree, they suddenly felt the heat and warmth that issued from the fire.   It was a delightful sensation,—the warmth they felt from fire.   Never had they felt it before, the delicious warmth of flames.

As the fire sank lower and lower, one of the smaller boys picked up a smoldering branch and whirled it in the air, but at that the branch cracked and sparkled and burst into sudden flame, which startled the child so thoroughly that he dropped his torch in surprise and it fell on a pile of dry leaves which readily caught fire, and made a merry blaze.

Thus Father discovered that fire had something to do with wood and dried leaves, and that he could keep it going if he would only feed it.   Gathering some smouldering branches, he took them into the cave and placed them carefully in a hollow of the rocks.   Then, kneeling before the blaze, he fed it with twigs and bits of wood until the flames leapt higher, and the smoke, curling up toward the roof, went out through the little cracks.   What a comfortable warmth filled the cave! Father knew that his fire would live. Henceforth he could keep his family comfortable and warm even on the coldest days.

And now there were four important things that the family knew how to use: clothing, the cave, the stone fist hatchet, and fire.   All of these came in the Early Stone Age, an immensely long period, lasting at least 100,000 years, during which the progress of man was very, very slow.

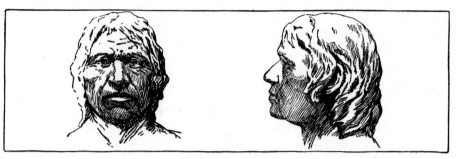

A front view and a side view of the Cro-Magnon man, so called because the first skull of this type of man was found in Cro-Magnon, France. Teeth were missing in the skull, and after they were restored, the anthropologist modeled the flesh, skin and hair so that people today might have a reproduction of a man of the Cro-Magnon race.

II

A Tall Race of Hunters Appears in Europe

Middle Stone Age

(About 30,000 b.c.—10,000 b.c.)

At last, the world had grown warmer. When the hard, stinging snow ceased, the sun coming out again, began to melt the thick ice in the valleys; and the water, thus set free, rushed down the mountain sides in a mighty flood, forming rivers and many lakes.

Grass, flowers, and trees began to thrive with strength, and it was not many years until the fresh green of growing things covered even the brown, bare spots where the ice had been before. There was still a cold season, but it was the same kind of winter weather as there is today, and this was followed by Spring, Summer, and Autumn in regular order. Indeed, from the days of the Fourth Glacial Period, when the ice formed and then melted, there have been no changes in climate.

Some 20,000 years after this flood, the primitive hunter folk had disappeared from Europe. In their place was the

25

tall, handsome Cro-Magnon race of well-built, intelligent men who came swarming into the land from some place to the south and eastward.

And now changes came more quickly. The slow upward struggle of the Old Stone Age was passed; for this tall handsome race of hunters was gifted and alert, far in advance of the low-browed, chinless, savage, Neanderthal men.

The Cro-Magnon men discovered how to make better clothes by cutting pieces of skin and sewing them together. They had learned that meat cooked over fire tastes better than meat eaten raw. They had found they could make a new fire whenever their old one went out, by rubbing a hard stick in soft rotted wood till a tiny flame appeared; they had better weapons, sharper knives, and spears with points of flint fastened to a wooden shaft by means of tough strips of leather. Above all, they had a language and could talk with each other freely.

At first, each separate family had found its own name for things, had made whatever sounds it chose to indicate an object, but these men met in groups to hunt, so they had to agree on some common words which all could understand if they were to work together. Thus

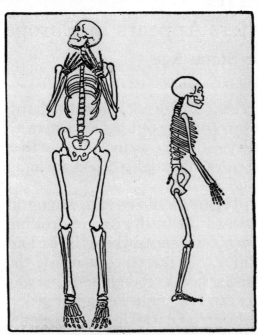

These two skeletons of men who lived in the Old Stone Age and the Middle Stone Age show why this chapter is called "A Tall Race of Hunters Appears in Europe." The smaller skeleton is that of a Neanderthal man found in the cave of La Chapelle-aux-Saints (see page 19). The taller skeleton is a man of the Cro-Magnon race found in the Grotte des Enfants. All Cro-Magnons were quite tall, the average height being six feet one and one-half inches.

Many years passed before early man learned how to make fire. At first fire was always taken from something set burning through natural causes and whenever the fire in the cave went out it was started again by carrying a flaming brand from some such source. Then men noticed that flint struck on any piece of rock which contained small bits of metal, produced a spark which would ignite punk or dried leaves. Still later men discovered that the friction caused by rubbing a hard wooden stick in the soft, rotten punk of a tree would cause the punk to smolder and finally burst into flame.

a crude form of language slowly developed among them.

People also had names, and these were usually given them because of some characteristic. In the cave where Father and the family had lived so many years before, there was now a tall handsome boy of this fine Cro-Magnon race and he had been called Og, because he never cooed and murmured like other babies, but instead said "Og-og-og-og," as he stumbled among the skins and played with bits of stone. His sister was straight and slender like the reeds which grew near the river and so

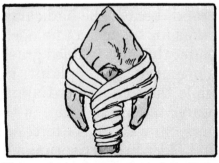

Flint arrow heads and spear heads were fastened to the wooden shafts by splitting the wood, inserting one end of the stone, and then making all tight by binding leather thongs around stone and stick.

The Cro-Magnon people lived not only in France, but also in northern Spain, and these funny little men were found painted upon the walls of one of the Spanish caves, where they have been since between 18,000 B.C., and 10,000 B.C. Although they were very crudely drawn, it is easy to see that they are intended to represent men. The purpose in drawing them is not known; perhaps they stood for enemies whom the magicians and sorcerers were to destroy by spells and enchantments, or perhaps they were simply pictures.

she was named River Reed. The Father was called Thrower because he could throw his spear farther than other men, and the Mother could run so swiftly that she had been rightly named Fleet Foot.

Og Invents the Bow and Arrow

Og lay on a pile of skins in a corner of the cave, waiting for the meat which River Reed was cooking. He had just returned from his first hunt with the men and he was tired, but proud, because he had carried his own flint spear and had asked for the help of no one. He had tramped over hill and plain, through tangled grass and prickly bush with never a murmur nor a complaint. He had lain quietly in the bushes while the feeding herd approached, wandering nearer and nearer the hiding place of the hunters, and he had thrown his spear with all the force of his arm, when his father, uncle and older brother sprang all at once to their feet to thrust their weapons suddenly at the unsuspecting beasts.

And now as he lay on his pile of skins, he played with the

stone-pointed spear which belonged to him alone.   Og could
throw straight and true when he was not too excited; he had
practiced day after day in the forest near the cave, but, because he was still very young, his throw did not have back
of it the strength for which he longed.

This fact bothered Og.   He thought a great deal about it,
and again he went over all the details of that day's great
adventure.

How long they had lain in the bushes till the grazing herd
came near enough for the hunters' spears to reach them!
Ah, could they only have thrown their spears when they first
sighted the beasts!   But to hurl a weapon so far would take
a great deal more force than the strongest hunter possessed.

This was what Og was thinking when River Reed inter-
rupted him with a call that his meat was ready.   As he
hurriedly rose to his feet, his spear dropped to the floor
with its head caught in the stones.   Bending over to get it,
he stumbled and almost fell, and his pressure against the
spear shaft bent it into a bow.   Stretched to its utmost, the

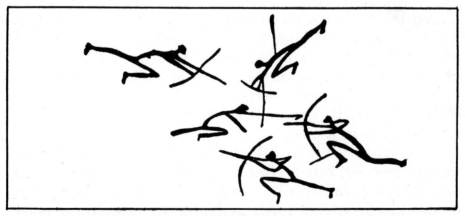

Upon the walls of a rock shelter in eastern Spain, men of the New Stone Age painted this exciting battle scene, called
"The Fight of the Bowmen."   The straight lines for bodies, arms and legs, and the round dots for heads are very
much like the pictures children draw.   The wonderful thing about this painting, however, is the vigor and spirit
which the artist has put into every movement.   In looking at the painting, it is possible to catch the very strain
and heat of a real fight.   It was probably made about 8,000 B.C.

About fourteen thousand years ago, this picture of a browsing reindeer was carved upon a piece of reindeer antler by a Cro-Magnon artist living near what is now Kisslerloch in Switzerland. The proportions of the reindeer are fine, and no modern artist could follow more closely or accurately the natural position of the animal with its head lowered to the grass. The most important thing about this carving, however, is the fact that it is the very earliest picture known showing landscape. The reindeer seems to be feeding beside a pool of water, shown by the wide dark lines. To the left, the upright lines are reeds growing in the pool near the shore, and there are even reeds shown upside down below the dark lines, giving a perfect idea of the reflection upon the surface of the water. Truly it is a remarkably life-like picture to have been drawn about 12,000 B.C.

wood sprang back, lifting the stone where its head was caught and throwing it with tremendous force clear across the cave. Crack! the stone whizzed through the air just missing River Reed. And River Reed was so startled that she almost dropped the meat.

For a moment Og was bewildered. There lay the spear at his feet, but whence had come all that force that had hurled the stone such a distance?

As he ate, he continued to wonder, and, pressing his spear against the ground, he noted with eager interest the strength of the push exerted against his hand when he bent the shaft in a bow. Then, with a strip of cured hide, he tied the two ends together, so the shaft could not straighten out but must remain in a bow.

What a new thing was this! Og was delighted with what he had learned, but he did not yet know how to use the force that was in his bow. The hide string hummed when he plucked it, giving forth agreeable sounds, so Og tried different methods of making that pleasant noise. Picking up a splinter of wood from the floor where his uncle had formed a spear shaft, he rubbed it across the string, amusing himself with the humming, until one end of the splinter caught in the hairs of the hide.   Then, as Og jerked to free it, pulling on the string, the splinter slipped from his fingers, and whizz! it shot through the air just as the stone had done.

"Hi!" cried Og in delight and he picked up another splinter and tried to make that fly. Soon, by investigation, he learned that his bit of wood could always be sent across the cave, if he placed it against the string, then pulled back the string and let it go again.

Without knowing it, Og had discovered what men in other parts of the world were learning at the same time, the principle of the bow and arrow.

At first, Og thought his bow nothing more than a toy, with which he and River Reed played in a glade on the edge of the forest; but, as he watched the splinter fly, he gradually came to see that here was the very thing for which he had been wishing, a weapon to throw a spear from a distance, and throw it with very great force.

With this idea in mind, Og made new bows of different woods, until he found just the springiness which threw his sticks the farthest. Then he made arrows, slender and straight, flint-pointed like his spear, but lighter and much shorter. Thus equipped,

A vigorous dancing warrior painted upon the rock shelter of Alpera, Spain, probably about 10,000 B.C.

Armed with bows and arrows, the hunters are shown shooting at the stags. This painting by early man is in dark red and appears upon the walls of the rock shelter of Alpera in Spain, where it has been since about 10,000 B.C. With feet spread apart to brace themselves, the hunters are drawing back their bows. Extra arrows are shown behind one of the hunters, and from the line stuck into one of the stags it would seem that at least one shot had found its mark.

he and River Reed practiced shooting in the forest until they were both good marksmen, but they told no one about their new weapon.

Not until Og was quite sure of his aim, did he take his bow one morning and go to the hunt with the men. How River Reed longed to go with them! But she waved a good-bye from the hill near the cave and Og knew how deep was her interest in what he should do that day.

"What is that thing, Og?" the boy's older brother asked when he saw what Og was carrying.

"It's something I made to hunt with," said Og and no one questioned further; for they naturally thought that Og was carrying nothing more than a toy.

It was a long, weary march over rolling plains, before the little band saw a herd of small deer, grazing quietly in the distance. Here was the food they sought, if only they could get close enough to throw their spears at the creatures.

At once they entered the forest, and, keeping near the edge, they crept up toward their prey, till they came to the end of the woodland, where they met keen disappointment; for the deer were still so far away that even with the longest spear-throw, no one could hope to reach them. Moreover, deer were so quick and alert, that should anyone show himself beyond the screen of the trees, they would all be off in an instant, far beyond hope of capture. Here was Og's chance at last to try his new bow and arrow.

"I can throw a spear farther than the deer," the boy said to his father, as the older men talked together, vainly seeking some way of securing the food which lay just out of their reach.

Og's father paid no heed. He did not deign to answer.

"I can do it with this thing," Og insisted, showing his bow to the men.

But no one bothered to look. They did not think his words worthy of even the least attention. So Og stepped up to the edge of the forest, and found a level space where he could stand well braced with his feet spread wide apart. Carefully choosing the straightest and sharpest of his arrows, he fitted it to the string. Then he drew back the bow, and, selecting the nearest group of deer, which grazed apart from the rest with heads buried deep in the grass, he sighted for the shot.

"Twang!" went the string. Swift flew the arrow; and down went a deer, while the herd bounded off in a flash.

The men were

Another painting of a stag hunt found upon the walls of the "Cueva de los Caballos" near Albocacer, Spain, dated about 10,000 B.C. This is also in dark red. Something seems to have driven a whole herd of reindeer toward the hunters, for the animals are rushing forward in spite of the arrows shot into them.

The large figure of the hunter on the right of this wall painting from the Cueva de la Vieja at Alpera, Spain, shows a feathery head-dress very much like that worn by the American Indians. The two figures to the left also have a head-dress. The arrows shown have only a single barb on the point, and although some have feathers on the shafts, others seem to be perfectly plain. This was painted at the end of the Middle Stone Age, about 10,000 B.C.

struck dumb with surprise. They stood absolutely speechless, watching open-mouthed, while Og ran into the open space to bring back the fallen deer.

At last men had discovered the use of the bow and arrow. They had taken a great step forward; for heretofore they had fought with beasts only at close range, depending on stealth or brute strength. Now they could substitute skill for strength. They had begun to think and to lift themselves, by their thinking, above the level of beasts.

The Beginning of Painting

One of the caves near that where Og and River Reed lived was a great deal larger than the others, so much larger, indeed, that in it several families lived with plenty of room and to spare. These families were all related, because each son, when he took a wife, had brought her home to an unused part of the big cave, instead of finding a smaller cave where they would be alone. An active old father, too, dwelt here, and he was head of the family, as fathers were in those days, no matter how old they were. Some forty people

lived there,—five sons and their families, with children of
all ages,—but sons and sons' wives and grandchildren all
obeyed the old father instantly and unquestionably, whatever he might say.

The boys and girls from this cave played with Og and
River Reed, and Og had among them one special friend, a
boy of his own age, named Mo.

Now one of Mo's uncles, called Guff, was the artist of the
family, and he had taught the boy how to cut the outlines
of animals on the stone walls of the cave. Og was eagerly interested in the carvings made by Mo, and he often held the
torch while Mo, in some far-off corner, was cutting on the
wall. Indeed, Og sometimes tried to make the outlines
himself, but in this he never succeeded.

Guff now and then took the boys on journeys through
forest and plain to show them the beasts of the region and
to point out their characteristics. And always when they
returned, Guff bade Mo try his hand at cutting what he had
seen. Of course Mo was not permitted to work on the
precious ivory, which came from the tusks of the mammoth;

A man, followed by his wife, child and dogs, shooting an ostrich with bow and arrow. This carving upon the
Atlas rocks of northern Africa is practically life-size. It was made by scratching lines in the rock, or punching
holes with pointed flint stone, and then going over these scratches or holes again until wide, deep outlines were
cut clearly in the rock.

An Atlas rock carving of two buffalo with great wide-spreading horns, an ostrich, and a man with a bow, followed by his dog, evidently running away from them.   This carving was made at least 5,000 years ago and the kind of buffalo shown has entirely disappeared from earth, although its bones are found frequently.   The man seems to have an apron fastened around his waist; his hair is shaved at the sides and piled in a crest upon his head.

it was far too difficult a task to catch the mighty mammoth. Hunters had to lay traps, and even when a maddened beast had fallen into the trap, it took scores of men to kill him. Material so rare as ivory was for the best artists only. But Mo was permitted to carve on bone, on deer antlers and on the walls of his cave.

It was here on the walls of his cave that he carved the creatures he knew best, the reindeer and river salmon. But the fierce cave bear, and the sabre-tooth tiger, the terror of men and beasts, Mo had never seen and so he did not carve them. His pictures of the mammoth, too, and the mighty woolly rhinoceros were not especially good because he met them so seldom. The animals he knew well, he also carved very well, and of these he liked best to cut the picture of the bison, an animal like the buffalo, which roamed in great herds through the land.

One afternoon, when Og and Mo had grown to be young men, they followed a herd for hours and then came home again to carve what they had seen.

Og held the torch while Mo worked, but after a while he

grew tired of standing still doing nothing; so he idly picked up from the floor a torch all charred at the end. As he swung this to and fro, it hit the side of the wall and made a sooty black mark.

"Look, look, Mo!" cried Og. "See the marks I make."

So Mo took the stick himself and tried making marks on the wall. In broad sweeping outlines he had soon traced the figure of a bison.

"Isn't that easy!" he cried. "I must tell Guff about this. Making marks on the wall with a stick is certainly far quicker work than cutting them in with a knife."

And Guff was likewise pleased, when he saw the black marks of the stick. To show him how it worked, Mo drew another bison; then Guff had to draw a bison, and the two grew so eager over the new discovery that the wall was soon covered with a whole great herd of bison. Even Og's crude attempt was among them.

"That's fine," cried Og, as the little group stepped back to view the work in the flickering light of the torch. "But

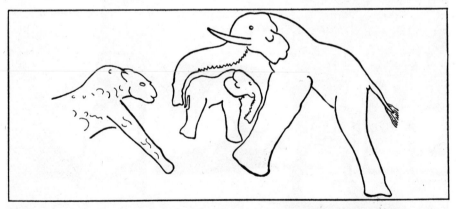

In this Atlas rock carving by early man a leopard is trying to carry off a baby elephant from beneath its mother's trunk where it has crawled for protection. The mother is angry. Her trunk raised to flay the leopard, her forefeet braced to receive the attack, she will fight to the end for her baby.   The drawing is so clear and full of action that the artist must have seen the very happening he cut in the rocks.   These African elephants are a good deal smaller than the Indian elephants seen frequently today.

I have another idea." And he disappeared from the cave.

In a moment he had returned, carrying in his hands a lump of yellow clay. "Try drawing with this," he said.

Guff covered a stick with the yellow clay, and now he found that he could also draw yellow lines on the wall.

Greatly excited, Og rushed out again, and this time he returned, bringing red and brown clay for the painting.

The drawings in this picture are copied from paintings made upon the walls of caves by men of the New Stone Age. The artist is shown in the act of drawing one of the bison found on the ceiling of Altamira, Spain. See page 39. The other animals—wild horse, reindeer, boar and wild steer—are from paintings in the cavern of Font de gaume Dordogne, France.

A little girl, five years old, found this beautiful painting of a bison on the ceiling of a cave near Altamira, Spain. Her father, the Marquis de Santuala, was interested in picking up pieces of flint, arrowheads, and other stones which early man had shaped and he and his daughter had gone into the cave together in search of these curious bits. After a time the child grew tired of watching her father dig. Being small, she could easily move about where the roof was too low for the man to stand upright. Suddenly she called out to him, "Toros! Toros!" This is Spanish for "Bulls! Bulls!" Her father came as quickly as he could and found her pointing up at the ceiling of the cave which was covered with paintings of animals, some of them being more than five feet long. Here were painted bison, stags, deer, horses, and wild oxen, together with pigs and wolves; all together, there were not less than eighty figures painted upon the ceiling. The bison here shown is one of the finest of these paintings; four shades of color were used, and in every detail it is remarkably true to life.

So Guff and Mo began filling in the black outlines of the bison with their red, brown, and yellow colors. They had found the first method of painting. They had, for the first time, used colors in making pictures of things.

Thus in the Middle Stone Age men learned how to paint as well as to carve. They discovered the bow and arrow and greatly improved their stone tools. Progress was still very slow but men were beginning to think, and to feel an inner impulse toward expressing themselves in art.

In this carving made by early man upon the Atlas Rocks of northern Africa, there is pictured a man wearing a mask with long ears, shaking his boomerang at a lion. Although out hunting for big game, the mask was just as important to the man as his weapon, for he undoubtedly thought that it would help him in overcoming the lion.

Quite often, when the earliest people went hunting for food, they would have their artists draw pictures of the animals they hoped to get. Sometimes these drawings had arrows sticking into them, and the people believed that the act of drawing the picture gave them some kind of magic power which made the success of their hunting sure. Probably most of the drawings of animals on the cave walls were made for this purpose.

Another way of bringing success in hunting was for one of the men to dress up in the skin of an animal. Then as he danced and sang a chant of magic words, the hunters knew they would be successful. The hunter in this picture has on only a part of an animal skin—the mask with long ears.

III

New Ways of Living

Late Stone Age or The Age of Polished Stone

(ABOUT 10,000 B.C.)

When men found out about fire and clothing, tools and a cave, long ago in the Early Stone Age, each family lived by itself. They had no friends or near neighbors; there was no one to share their joys, no one to help them. But now, in the Late Stone Age, people lived together. The children made friends with the children of other families, and the wives visited with one another, while the men went hunting in groups. And it is a good thing for people to be together. When they live apart, one man who is a thinker may discover something of real importance, which makes it easier to obtain food or prepare it; but unless other people hear of the new invention, it can be of little use except to that one family.

40

Therefore, as time went on, many changes in living and thinking slowly came about, but with no clocks or watches to measure hours, no calendars to measure time, year followed year, unnoticed, and

Here are some engraved outlines found upon cave walls, supposed to show masks used in bringing success in hunting, in finding favor with the gods, or for other magic purposes. They were carved about 18,000 B.C.

the Middle Stone Age grew into the Late Stone Age without any sudden change.

The most important development was the discovery that flint tools need no longer be made by prying off layers of stone which always left ragged edges, but could be given sharp, even edges, if they were ground on a whetstone, a hard stone with small sharp grains. The new period was therefore called the Age of Polished Stone.

Chisels, drills, saws, the stone ax, and the stone knife were now ground on a whetstone. Men had nearly as many tools as the carpenter of to-day, all made of stone, of course, but strong and sharp and serviceable. With these they could cut down whole trees and not merely the smaller branches. They could even cut other kinds of stone which were not as hard as flint. And so at last they were ready to make themselves better homes.

Instead of living in caves, they began to make little round huts, and this was very important because it shows

This drawing shows the priest, or medicine-man, or sorcerer, dressed up in the antlers, mask, beard, skin and tail of different animals, for the purpose of bringing good hunting to the men, or securing for them the favor of the gods. The painting is twelve feet from the floor of the cave of Trios Frères in the Pyrenees Mountains and was made about 15,000 B.C.

With the aid of their medicine-man, or sorcerer, a group of hunters are trying to work magic so that their next day's hunting may be successful. The sorcerer wears the antlers, head, skin, and tail of an animal like the sorcerer in the picture at the bottom of page 41. Some of the hunters wear magic masks, as shown in the upper picture page 41. As they dance about the fire, a hunter pretends to shoot the skin-clad sorcerer and this, it is believed, means that the animal the sorcerer represents will be killed without fail in the hunt next day. The feathered head-dress, bow and arrows of this hunter, as well as his air of vigorous dancing, are taken from the rock-painting, page 31. All primitive people believed in the power of magic and seldom went hunting without thus making success certain.

that people were becoming more and more masters of natural conditions, struggling to overcome the limitations they found in any part of the world. These earliest houses were round, and the framework was usually made of the reeds which grew in the marshes, over which there was a coating of thick mud. Such houses could be built wherever a family chose. Usually a circle of stones was placed around the walls within the hut; and at one side of the doorway, these stones were grouped together to form a place for the fire.

It did not take people long to build a hut like this, and so it was no great task to move about to new homes. Men could not thus move their caves, and if they chose to live in a cave, they had to stay in one place, even when the herds of animals wandered far away. So, gradually, there developed two different ways of living. Some people still lived in caves and had permanent dwelling places. Others wandered about, following the herds, and building new homes very frequently wherever they settled down.

It was in one of these reed and clay huts that a certain boy and girl once lived many thousands of years ago. Dee and his sister Dart were twins, and they lived by the grey North Sea, in the land that is now called Denmark.

The entire family had helped build the new house on a spot which the father Dorn had chosen not far from the shores of the sea. Dart was especially skillful at weaving the reeds back and forth, and she and her mother Durth had worked away at the framework, while Dee and his father, waist high in the marshes, had kept them supplied with rushes. Afterward, Dorn had plastered the hut with mud which the twins had brought him.

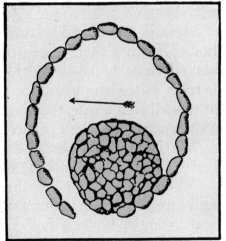

Plan of the remains of a late Stone Age hut. The circle of stones was placed around the walls of the hut. The open place at the left, was the door, and the solid circle of stones near the opening was the hearth. There were no chimneys in early huts, so the fire had to be built near the doorway to permit the smoke to escape.

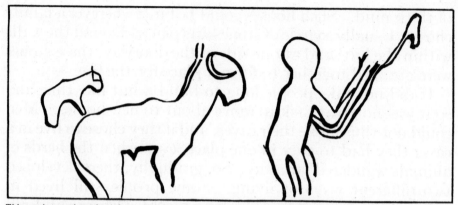

This carving cut into the Atlas rocks of northern Africa shows a man holding a stone ax in his hand, followed by sheep. The first axes did not have handles; men held them in their fists when they wished to cut or chop anything. But this picture was made after it had been learned that greater force could be given to the blow by attaching the stone ax blade to a long stick or wooden handle.

The First Pets

It was a very happy life which the four led in their little hut beside the grey-blue sea. There were other families close by, but food was always plentiful, wild duck from the marshes and sometimes wild boar or wild bull.

Most of the time Dee and Dart did not go very far from home, because there were wolves in the neighborhood. They stayed close to their mother, helping her pick fruits and berries, gathering wood for the fire, or searching for oysters and shell-fish along the shores of the sea. But sometimes, as a great treat, their father took them out hunting.

"Father," cried Dee one night as they all sat about the fire. "Take Dart and me with you tomorrow!"

"What does your Mother say?" asked Dorn, yawning and stretching his arms, for he had tramped far that day, and brought home a heavy bull.

"O Mother, let us go!" cried Dee and Dart together.

The Mother smiled on both children and readily gave her consent. So Dorn and his young son and daughter set out next morning at dawn, the children each carrying a bow with a small bag full of arrows and a sharp flint knife at the belt.

It was a bright, cloudless day, just cool enough for tramping. The three did little hunting, but, as they marched along, Dorn told them about the wolf and wild boar, where they hid and how to hunt them; he pointed out the ducks' nesting places, and showed them queer fish in the water. Then he made the twins hide in the tall grass or bushes, just as they would have done, had they really been out hunting.

It was mid-afternoon, on their way back home, when Dorn halted the children suddenly.

"Quiet!" he cautiously whispered, and Dee and Dart stood still, listening with both ears.

Soon they made out a whimper, the little crying yelp of animals close by.

Dorn crept slowly forward and disappeared in the grass. But in a few moments he called:

"Come here! Dee! Dart! Come here!"

One of the finest of the pictures upon the Atlas rocks is that of a wild ass with two young ones. The cutting of the outline of these animals is very firm and clear, the figures are well-proportioned and life-like, and a real artist with sincerity of feeling must have done the work.

Hurrying to him at once, the children found him seated and holding two little animals who yipped at him in suspicion.

"What are they?" cried Dart in surprise.

"Wolf pups," replied her Father. "Take one. They won't hurt you."

And he put one into the girl's arms and gave the other to Dee. "Hold them tight or they'll run!"

"Where is the mother?" asked Dee, for he knew the mother-wolf would not be very far from puppies as young as these.

"She must have been struck down by some hunter's arrow," said Dorn; "for she is nowhere about."

So the children played with the pups while Dorn sat watching them, smiling. At times one clumsy puppy would escape from the children's arms, and pretend to be glad he was free. He would shake himself and jump around, but he always seemed secretly anxious for the children to catch him again.

"O Father," cried Dart at last. "Let us keep these pups!"

Dorn was greatly astonished. Beasts were good for food, and their hides had many uses, but what could one possibly do with live wolf pups like these?

"I want to keep this one to play with." Dart explained.

So Dorn agreed and the children took the two young wolf cubs home.

"What have we here?" cried Durth, as much surprised as Dorn. "What can we do with wolf cubs?"

Nevertheless, she, too, in a short time loved the pups, and she helped the children feed them, and fastened them securely to pegs driven into the ground. They called the pups Goo and Gah, because they, too, were twins.

Day by day, as Dee and Dart played with the wolf cubs, they all became firm friends, and soon it was no longer necessary to fasten the pups to the pegs, for they always kept close to the children and were in and out of the hut, very much in Durth's way.

So that is how man found his first animal friend. And as time went on, and the wolves became more and more dog-like, they helped Dorn in his hunting and guarded the children from danger. When other men heard of Dorn's

This drawing of a wolf by the artists of the Middle Stone Age, about 10,000 B.C., was found upon the walls of the cave of Font-de-gaume in France. Unlike many other drawings, the animal was not traced in red, but in black. First, a part of the cave wall was smoothed down and this was then covered over with red crayon or paint. The outline of the wolf was afterwards drawn in black upon the red background, and certain parts were shaded in black to make the drawing look more natural.

useful pets, they also trained animal pups—wolves and the young of the jackal. Slowly these wild beasts changed until they became the dogs that man loves so dearly today.

Making Pots of Clay

Now Dee and Dart lived thousands of years ago in the Late Stone Age, and yet they were not very different from the children of today, especially in their games. Almost every afternoon, they could be found on the shore, wading and dabbling about and building little toy huts.

One day they made a lake by digging a hole in the mud, and they lined, with woven reeds, the channel which let in the water. Then they made a log bridge to place across the channel and when their task was done, they viewed it with real pride.

"Now we must make some houses," cried Dart, "for the people who live by the lake."

"All right," Dee agreed. So they set to work again, gathering more reeds and weaving little round huts which they covered over with mud. In the last gleam of light before dark, they had the pleasure of seeing a handsome little village placed all around their lake. And when Durth called them to come in and sleep, they were no more willing to go than children are today.

"O let us stay up a bit longer," they teased. "Just a little bit longer!"

Next day when they returned to their lake, the sun had baked the mud village until the houses were all so hard that they could be picked up and moved about wherever the children chose.

"Look, look!" cried Dee, holding a house upside down. "It's just like a basket, covered with mud. I think it would carry water."

And he stooped and filled the house from the sea. Sure enough, he had guessed aright! The water remained in the house, and not a drop leaked out.

Just then Mother Durth came down to the marsh and saw Dee carrying water in that strange sort of basket.

"What's that, Dee?" she cried. "How are you carrying water?"

So Dee showed his mother the basket and Durth ex-

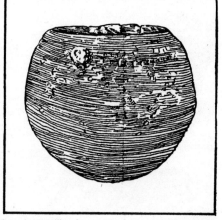

One of the earliest known pieces of pottery. The pot, or jar, was formed and shaped entirely by hand, so that it is rather clumsy and crude. It has no decoration except the marks cut into it when the clay was soft. These cuts were once filled with white chalk, which has since fallen out.

claimed, and murmured, and began to talk to herself: "Now just think of that! How long it is since people have known that the sun will bake clay hard, yet no one has ever thought before that baked mud might hold water."

And she went on thinking further. "If this mud basket holds water, perhaps I could use it in boiling meat instead of my heavy stone pot."

Now this stone pot, to which Durth referred, was found, in the Late Stone Age, in almost every home. To make it, the father of the family selected a great block of stone, and then with drills and flint chisels, he cut and chipped away, working at the inside, until he had made a hole large enough to hold several gallons of water. But this was such very hard work and took such a very long time that families rarely possessed more than one precious pot.

Moreover, these stone pots were heavy, and the walls were so thick that heat from outside could never pierce a way through. To cook in them, small stones were taken

and placed in an open fire. The pot was filled with water and meat, and when the stones were hot enough, they were thrown into the pot. As more and more stones were added, the water came to a boil, and some one had to watch the pot and keep throwing in more hot stones until the meat was done.

Durth knew that the mud basket, if only it would hold water, was thin enough to let heat pass through, and so could stand over the fire and would not have to be watched and constantly fed with stones. What a great deal of time would be saved if she could cook like this!

So she took the mud basket into the hut, filled it with water and pieces of meat and placed it over the fire.

But the mud had now been touched for such a long time by the water that it began to melt, turning soft again, and dripping water and mud slowly into the fire, which sputtered and almost went out.

That evening Durth told Dorn about her trial with the basket, how for a time it had held the water and then turned back into mud.

"If it would only stay hard," she said, "it would be a great help in cooking. I could place it right over the flames."

As she spoke, it chanced that Dorn, poking the coals of the fire, found there a large piece of mud which had dripped from the vanished basket. This he raked out with a stick, and when it had quite cooled off, he took it up in his hands and saw that it was hard, stone-like in every respect.

So he put this hard piece in the family stone jar, and filled the jar with water. All night the mud lay in the water, but in the morning, behold, it was still as hard as rock.

Now Dorn thought about this all day, and the more he thought, the surer he was that it was the effect of the fire which had changed the mud into stone.

So the next day he made a new basket, and after the sun had dried it, he built a big fire in the open and placed his

Right beside the fire place in this picture, there is a drawing of the kind of pot Durth used for boiling meat. A hole cut inside the solid stone was filled with water, and hot stones were put in it until the water boiled.

People always like to have beautiful things about them; so almost as soon as they had learned how to make pottery, they began decorating it by painting colored designs upon the soft clay before burning. This jug has straight up and down bands and a zigzag design.

basket squarely in the middle of the flames. Thoroughly he cooked it, and then when he scattered the wood, he found that his mud basket had become a hard stone pot, which would hold water for any time and could be used for cooking directly over the flames.

So it was Dee and Dart who made the hard mud basket, Durth who saw how helpful it would be in cooking, and Dorn who found out how to make the mud stay hard by baking it in the fire.

Then Dorn told other people how he had made his pot, and it was not long before everyone was making pots of clay. There were many different shapes, because mud was easily formed and molded when it was soft, and scores of new uses were found for these convenient vessels.

Soon, too, someone learned that mud could be painted before it was baked, and fire would bake the paint so that it would not wash off; and because people like to have pretty things around them, most of the pottery after this was decorated in some way with different designs and colors.

As people became more skillful in painting designs upon pottery, they were able to draw the more graceful spiral patterns. The picture shows several pieces of pottery with different treatments of spiral designs.

Now, living in huts instead of caves, with animals for friends, with plenty of polished stone tools and pottery to make work easier, all meant that the people of the Late Stone Age were rapidly progressing and leading more secure and comfortable lives.

IV

The Lake Dwellers

Late Stone Age

Dorn had heard of a people who knew how to make better houses than the mud hut in which he lived. One of his neighbors, a younger man, had journeyed into the South a few years before, and he had many wonderful tales to tell of different ways of living. He told of a people who not only built their houses from the trunks of trees, but who caught fish with hook and line instead of spearing them, as Dorn had always done, standing for hours on the bank, patiently waiting to cast his spear, whenever he saw the flash of a shadowy fin in the water.

Dorn was greatly interested. Durth was also impressed, and sometimes she would tell him that they really should go South and try to find out for themselves about these new ways of living. And so they decided at length to make the journey southward.

Dorn gathered together his skins, and his stone tools. And then he asked the children to which of their friends they meant to give their wolf cubs.

"We can't part with Goo and Gah," the twins began to wail; so their father was forced to agree that the pets should go along with them.

One bright spring morning, the family said good-bye to their neighbors and set

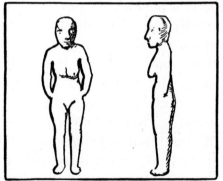

The earliest artists not only carved and painted figures of people and animals, but they also molded and cut out of stone or ivory beautiful little figures. The figure shown in the picture was made in Egypt about fifteen thousand years ago.

53

forth on their journey,—a real journey of discovery, in-
spired by the eager desire to find out what men had
learned in countries far away.

On the second day, they passed beyond the land which
Dorn knew from his hunting, and thenceforth they set their
course by the sun, going slowly but surely southward.

The wolf pets ran and scampered close beside the twins.
It was all a glorious adventure. Sometimes the family
spent a week beside a flowing river, or on the banks of a
limpid lake, while Dorn went hunting in the neighborhood
to lay in supplies of meat.

On these occasions, a small mud hut would be erected or
a simple leaning roof to protect them from the weather.
Here Durth would cook and attend to her regular duties,
and although the twins were never permitted to go beyond
her sight, they played with the cubs, with pebbles and
leaves in their usual happy manner.

The sun shone brightly most of the time, and each day
grew longer and warmer; so they frequently rested at noon-
day, and then continued their journey as long as the light
remained. Gradually, the land changed. After wading
across a shallow place in a very wide, rushing river, the
family found themselves at length in the midst of a rolling,
green plain, where there were not as many thick forests as
there had been in their old land, and where there were
many different kinds of gay-colored flowers and birds.

Sometimes they came to villages built down close to the
water. Then Dorn would leave his family hidden carefully
in the bushes and go forward with open arms and hands to
show that he was a friend. In general, the villagers received
the newcomers with kindness and fed them with strange
new cooked meats, or with different herbs, and berries.
Sometimes Durth and Dorn had difficulty in making them-

selves understood, because their language was not exactly like that of the village people, but signs always helped them out and they got along very well.

Dorn was a bit disappointed to find the houses in this new land still made of woven reeds, like the ones he knew how to build, except for the use of small tree trunks to support the walls and roof; but Durth, one day, learned something that to her was very important. She heard of a new kind of food.

Now up to the time when the family had started out on their journey, they had lived on meats and fish almost entirely, and there were not many different kinds of meat from which to choose. About the only variety was in the method of cooking. Meat might be held on spits and roasted over the fire, or baked in the coals, or boiled in a pot of water. The only other food beside meat was herbs, fruits, nuts, and berries.

But to these usual foods about which everyone knew, the women of the river villages added a wonderful treat,—a kind of bread, made from ground berries of wheat which grew wild in the plain nearby.

The powder of this wheat was mixed with water and formed into thick round cakes, which were then cooked on flat stones heated in the fire. This was the first bread that people made, and Durth noted every step carefully. She learned that the wheat must be a ripe gold before picking. The village women showed her the exact amount of water used in the mixture and how to test the cooking to be sure that the bread was done. And when the travellers started southward again, Durth carried with her a jar of powdered wheat which the village women had given her.

For days the family noted that the country grew more rolling and they seemed to be mounting higher. Then, one morning, Dorn called attention to a gray-blue mass far off that seemed a bank of clouds. As they journeyed nearer, however, they saw that the mass of clouds was really a range of mountains, rising blue and misty against the line of the sky.

But here they were stopped by a river, broad, and swiftly flowing, wider and deeper than any they had crossed before. Dorn was obliged to spend several days chopping trees and making a raft, while Dee helped bind the logs together with the tough, strong stalks of vines. Then the jars and bundles, carried on the journey, were placed in the center of the raft. The family sat down beside them, and Goo and Gah were fastened with leather strips to the floor. Father cut the vine which held the raft to the shore, and so the family entrusted themselves with all their worldly possessions to the mercy of the stream.

Dorn had a long pole which he stuck in the bottom of the river, intending to direct the raft straight to the opposite shore, but the strength of the current was far too great. Westward, it bore the little bark, and with such tremendous force that Dorn could no longer guide it. The family found themselves afloat, alone on the face of the waters, swirling, pitching, dipping, and helplessly borne away, in a different direction entirely from the one they had wished to take. Sometimes the raft scraped so close to the rocks, that the travelers held their breath and clung to each other for safety, while the wolf pups crouched still lower and whimpered in fright. And once it tipped so dangerously that Goo slipped down to the very edge and was only kept by the strip of hide from falling into the river.

Through all the long hours of the day, the exciting journey continued, but just as the sun was setting, the raft swept around a bend and headed straight toward a sandy beach. Then Dorn found bottom with his pole and was able at last to guide his bark safely to the shore.

Ah, what a relief it was to feel dry ground beneath their feet! Thankfully the family laid themselves down to sleep beneath the stars.

Next morning they set out southward again. They had no means of knowing how far to the west they had drifted, but each day brought the mountains nearer to their view, rugged, snow-peaked, glistening.

The country grew more wooded, and soon they plunged into forests, shadowy and mysterious, with tall, straight, soaring tree-trunks and interlacing branches, through which the sun came trickling in flitting gleams of gold. Then, at length, one afternoon, they came on the shores of a lake, so wide they could scarcely see across, and here they made their encampment and rested for the night.

After their experience on the river, Dorn did not wish to attempt a crossing of the lake. It was necessary, therefore, to walk around the water; but on the following morning, when the journey was continued, the family suddenly rounded a jagged mass of rocks, and saw, all at once, the very thing for which they had sought so long, a village of wooden houses.

"Look!" cried Dee, almost gasping. "The houses are in the water!"

And they all stood still in amazement, for the village certainly did appear to float on the face of the lake. But as they drew nearer, creeping cautiously through the forest, they saw that the houses rested on wooden platforms, which were supported by piles, driven down into the soil at the bottom of the lake. From each of these wooden platforms, a small bridge led to the shore.

"You wait here in the forest," said Dorn, whispering to Durth and the children, "while I step out on the beach and make myself known to the people."

Then he stepped from the protection of the trees, and with open arms, walked slowly toward the nearest bridge. Almost at once, however, a sudden shout arose. A man rushed out of a house, ran to the edge of the bridge and pulled on a dangling rope. Instantly, a part of the bridge was lifted up in the air, and a stretch of open water lay between Dorn and the Lake Dweller. Then other men ap-

The mud hut home of Durth and Dorn was in Denmark on the shore of the North Sea. By travelling straight south, they moved through Germany, following first the Elbe River and then the Weser River where they were carried away by the current, arriving finally at the lake village off the shore of Lake Constance in Switzerland.

The lake-dwellers cut down trees with their stone axes, chopped off the branches, and so made piles twenty feet long sharpened at one end. These piles were driven several feet into the bottom of the lake where the water was eight or ten feet deep. Upon the platform which was supported by the piles, they then built their houses using rough boards for the sides and reeds for the thatched roof. Railings were placed all around and a small bridge gave passage to the shore. Sometimes several houses were built upon one platform, but when separate platforms were built, they were all connected by narrow passageways.

peared, lining up on the platform, all armed with spears, with bows and arrows, and axes.

Dorn stood perfectly still till he noticed that one of the men, who seemed to be the leader, motioned him to come closer.

"What do you want?" the man called.

The language was not just like Dorn's, but, still, it was close enough so that he could understand.

Slowly and carefully, he explained that he and his family were traveling alone, that he did not wish to make war, but had only come to visit and to learn new ways of living.

Dorn then called to Durth, and the family appeared on

the beach, laden with jars and bundles. As soon as the Lake Dwellers realized that the newcomers were not enemies, but only peaceful visitors, they let down the break in the bridge and received them with greatest kindness.

The leader explained to Dorn that the houses were built in the lake so there would be greater protection from roving bands of robbers or wild beasts in search of food.

"Bears sometimes attack huts on land," he said; "but out here over the water, they are never able to reach us."

Now the Lake Dwellers had made better use of their flint tools than had the people of Dorn's old country, and the houses themselves were fashioned in a manner very different from the mud hut. A framework of rough timber was first erected in a square or rectangular form, and to this boards were fastened with wooden pegs. Mud was plastered in the cracks and thus the entire building was lasting, tight and strong. Openings were left for doors, and some of the houses had window holes high up near the roof, which was sloping and thatched with grass. Most of the houses had porches and the roofs were extended to cover these porches just as they did the house.

Inside, the houses had tables, stools, and benches made of wood, and there were wooden pitchers and spoons, besides fine pottery vessels.

One of these lake dwellings happened to be empty when

The Swiss Lake Villages were discovered in 1854 when a long dry season caused the water in the lakes to become quite low. Then it was that piles such as these were noticed sticking up from the bottom, and in the mud around the piles there were found pottery, bits of cloth, tools, furniture, ornaments and other personal belongings.

All that remains of a real dug-out canoe belonging to early man. Made by hollowing the trunk of an oak tree.

Dorn and Durth arrived, and in this the family made their home.

Soon the newcomers had become a real part of the village. Dorn went hunting with the men and learned how to make a boat, a "dug-out," as it was called, because it was made of the trunk of a tree which had been dug out inside. Durth worked with the women, and the twins learned to fish from their own front porch, using a fish-hook of bone fastened to a hide string and baited with bits of flesh.

How Dart Began Farming

Now, one of Dart's duties, as she grew a little older, was the gathering of the golden wheat berry used in making bread. Early each morning she left the house, bearing her pottery jar, and all day long she searched for the wheat in the broad, rolling plains about. Sometimes Dee would go with her; but more often she went with the girls of the village who had the same task as she.

What a great deal of time it took! Sometimes the little wheat-gatherers would find a large patch of grain, where they could pick berries for several days, but more often the plants were scattered in among other grasses and they could pick but a handful before going on with their search.

All through the summer Dart worked, and her wheat

was stored in pottery jars against the cold winter weather, when the grass-lands would all be brown and there would be no more berries.

It was on one of these wheat-gathering days, that something happened of tremendous importance to all the villagers. Dee had gone with Dart, and as they neared home in the late afternoon, bearing their well-filled jars, they were playing a game of tag. Usually Dart was the swifter, so that Dee had to dodge about to keep from getting caught, and on this particular afternoon, as he tried to slip out of her reach, he fell with a headlong plunge, and spilled his precious wheat in a shower all over the ground.

At that, the game stopped at once, and both the children flung themselves down to pick up their golden treasure. But they could not recover it all. In their frantic efforts to get back every single grain, they only pressed some of the berries well down into the ground.

For several weeks after this, Dart did not pass that way;

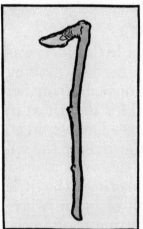

but when she chanced once again to come on the scene of their mishap, she found that the rich black soil where Dee had spilled the seed was covered with short green plants that looked very much like grass. Early in the following spring, each of these plants lifted bearded heads, laden with golden berries, and as Dart set herself to gather them, she thought, with a sigh of relief, what a help it was to have the plants all growing there in one place.

A hoe belonging to the Late Stone Age. It was made from a bit of branch with a sharp angle in it, and the flint stone-head was fastened into the split wood by wrapping around it many layers of leather thong.

Now this was the very first time that anyone had planted seed for grain, and though Dee and Dart had by no means

The hoe used by Dart in preparing the ground is exactly like the real hoe shown on page 62.

intended to do such a thing, Dart often thought of the matter during the summer which followed, and when she remembered how the seed had been spilled and pressed down into the earth, how the plants had grown and given new seed, she began to see very clearly that men might sow seed by intention and grow their grain in one spot, instead of depending entirely on chance, and being compelled to hunt for it all over the plains round about. So she talked with her father and mother about her new idea, and they gave her permission to try and see what she could do.

During the winter of course, she could do nothing whatever, save talk about the planting; but what she hoped to accomplish, gave rise to so much discussion, that by the time spring had returned, everyone in the village was curious and eagerly interested in the outcome of her attempt.

Dee made her a kind of hoe which was nothing more than an ax-blade attached to an extra long handle. And with this simple instrument and Dee at hand to help her, Dart set to work on her field.

It was not a large patch they planted, but they broke the ground very thoroughly and pressed the seed into the soil with a great deal of care. Then as the weather grew warmer and the grain plants pushed up their heads, Dart

This is a mealing stone, or grinder for breaking up the grain into meal, or flour. It was simply a rough piece of stone hollowed out to hold the grain, and another small, smooth stone was used for crushing.

cut out the weeds and carefully tended her plants, until at last in midsummer the berries began to appear.

How delighted was Dart! One day she filled her jar and brought her first berries home in triumph, while a crowd of chattering on-lookers followed at her heels.

Then Dart ground the grain between two stones, Durth mixed the powder with water to form the cakes, and placed them on the hot stones to cook. And that evening, when Dee and Dorn came home from hunting, they ate the bread made from the seed that Dart had learned how to grow.

Thus it was that Dart began farming; and next year the other villagers each selected a piece of ground and planted wheat seed, likewise. Little did Dart then dream of what a great thing she had done, but, as every one took up farming, the effects in years to come were very far-reaching, indeed.

When each family had a small piece of ground upon which they grew their grain, they could not move about and wander from place to place as Dorn and Durth had done, without depriving themselves of the harvest. It took all summer for the plants to grow, and the fields must be tended and kept free of weeds. This meant that families were now compelled to settle down in one place, so that after farming began, people did not move about nearly as much as before. And as the same family, year after year, plowed and cultivated the very same piece of ground, they gradually came to think of that land as belonging solely to them. And so the idea of owning land arose from farming also.

More land was planted, not with wheat berries only, but also with other seeds, until at length, instead of depending solely on hunting and fishing for food, men provided for their families by spending more time in farming.

Dart Learns How to Make Cloth

It happened one day when Dart was roaming about the plains, that she flung herself down to rest beside some tall slender plants with beautiful blue flowers. She had noticed these plants before, and now she lazily plucked one, beginning absent-mindedly to pick away at its stem.

The stem came apart very easily, dividing, beneath her fingers, into long, thin fibers on which she was dreamily pulling. But slowly she woke to the fact, that, although she was pulling with force, the fibers refused to break. Their strength was truly amazing, far greater indeed than their size and appearance had indicated.

Then Dart sat up and took notice. She twisted three or four of the long, tough fibers together, and lo, she had in her hands a fine, long flaxen thread on which she could pull very hard without being able to break it. And, being a keen and alert young girl, always actively thinking, she no sooner had the thread than she began to wonder at once if she could not somehow use it.

Frequently Dorn had complained to her that the hide thongs attached to his fish-hooks became very hard and rough when dry, and were difficult to handle. So Dart determined to make a fish line of her thread. Plant after plant of the blue-flowered flax she gathered, and patiently she labored to separate the fibers that formed the slender stalk. These she twisted together, adding new fibers to lengthen the thread, until it was long enough to serve as a fishing line. Then she found that, no matter how long the

thread remained in the water or lay exposed to the sun, it was always soft and flexible.

Dorn was enthusiastic over what Dart had found, and soon all the village was making and using flaxen fishing lines. And the next Spring, Dart planted flax as well as wheat in her garden.

One day Dorn said to Dart:

"The lake is so full of fish that I have been wondering if we could not make a sort of basket of this new thread, so that we could scoop up a lot of fish at a time."

"I'll try," said Dart. And she set to work at once.

As Dee saw her twisting the fibers slowly with her hands, and noted how much time it took and how much care and pains, he thought of an idea to make the twisting easier. Securing a small piece of clay, he moulded it into a flattened ball and pierced it with a hole. After he had baked this in the fire until it was hard, he pushed several lengths of the fiber through the hole, and knotted these on the opposite side. Then holding the loose ends at arm's length, he gave the ball a swing. Rapidly, the fibers twisted themselves together, and the thread was more firm and even than Dart could make with her hands.

"How splendid!" cried Dart in delight, for Dee had discovered spinning. The flat clay ball, used in twisting the thread, is called a spinning whorl, and with it Dart progressed rapidly in making her fishing net. On the very day when the net was finished, Dorn and Dee used it to drag in a whole school of floundering silver fishes.

Now Dart had become by this time so deeply interested in flax, that she constantly sought for new ways of making use of her threads. One day she decided to make a flaxen basket.

Laying a number of long threads in parallel rows on the floor, she began weaving another thread back and forth between them, just as she did in making a basket of reeds. But the threads on the floor would not lie straight, like reeds, and this made it very difficult to weave thread in between them. Accordingly, she asked Dee to make her a wooden frame with little pegs at the sides, to which she could fasten the parallel threads; and when she sat down before this frame, the threads were held so straight and tight, that she could easily weave her long thread in and out between them. And thus there began to grow on her frame, not the flaxen basket she had intended, but the very first piece of cloth,— coarse and uneven in spots, here woven too tight and there too loose, but still the very first cloth.

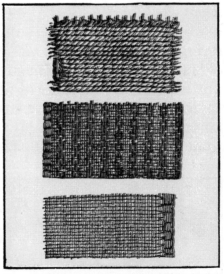

Many small pieces of cloth made by the lake-dwellers were found in the mud beneath the piles, and these three samples show how perfectly the early people wove the flaxen threads into cloth.

This was one of the greatest discoveries since farming; it really helped to make farming still more of an occupation, because man could now raise in his own fields both food and clothing, the two necessities of life, which he had heretofore been able to secure by no other means than hunting. No longer was he dependent on chance. Whether or not he brought home much game, he and his family could always henceforth be comfortably clothed and fed.

So the people of the lake village gradually changed their method of living, and the new life of waving fields beside the blue waters of the lake was far more peaceful than the old savage life of hunting.

In addition to their cultivation of the land, the Lake Dwellers also tamed some of the wild animals of the neighborhood, sheep, and goats, and cattle, and the cattle were soon taught to draw a rude plow through the fields.

Then a crude form of government arose. In the days when each family lived alone, the father or the mother had made important decisions and been obeyed by all, and when several sons' families lived together, it was usually the old, old father who acted as their chief. But when many families, not related, began to form little villages, they had to turn to some one to settle whatever differences might arise among them. Therefore, by general consent, they selected some man as chief because of his wisdom and justice, and the

Wall paintings from Si-er'ra Mo-re'na, Spain, showing that men of the Late Stone Age had tamed a number of animals. Three men lead horses or asses by halters. Next to the central man is a small animal which seems to be a cat. At the right an affectionate couple, hand in hand, walk beside a hunter with a bow. Painted about 10,000 B.C.

The stag hunt. A lively chase painted in dark red in the "Cueva del Mas d'en Josep" near Albocacer, Spain, and belonging to the Late Stone Age, about 10,000 B.C. The hunter wears three feathers in his hair, and feathers are attached at his waist and knees. He has shot two arrows into the deer, and is doing his best to keep up with the wounded animal. The excitement and action of the hunt are depicted with remarkable spirit.

villagers gave him authority and abided by his decisions.

And so it came about that when a really wise man governed a village, other men liked to come and live beneath his rule. Thus some of the villages began to grow larger and larger until they became thriving towns. Then many people stopped farming and each made his living by working at his own particular craft.

Naturally, some men were better at furniture-making than others, and people came to such a man and offered him grain or cattle to make them tables and chairs. Gradually this man gave more and more time to furniture making, and less and less to farming; until at length he became a craftsman only and did no more work in the fields. This method of exchanging grain for furniture, or cattle for pottery, was the beginning of trade, or business; and it was carried on, not only between people, but even between whole towns and villages.

A rock carving from Lake O-ne′ga in North Russia showing an enormous giant over ten feet high. This carving was made by early man so many thousands of years ago that no date can be given it. In later times, a simple-minded Russian peasant, believing this giant to be a devil, and thinking that he had caused some evil which had befallen the peasant's village, carved the cross over the devil's hand to deprive him of his power.

In certain localities, it was found that the flint stone was better than in others, and men would come from villages far away to trade for this good stone. Then the town where the stone was found, began to pay more and more attention to its stone-pits; till commerce in stone became its special business.

Moreover, as people began to live in towns, so that many could work together, another improvement developed. They were able to build earthen walls to shut in their groups of houses and protect them from strange, wandering tribes, who appeared now and then to pillage.

In time, men learned to make stone structures and stone tombs for the dead, shaping the stones very carefully with no rough, uneven edges, and cutting them to a size.

Of course, all these changes did not come about at once, but were worked out very slowly. Fifty thousand years passed between the time when hunters first found they could make fist hatchets, and the time when people lived in towns and made buildings out of stone. It was a very slow process indeed, growing from hunting to farming, from cave dwelling to hut dwelling; but henceforth men went forward with ever increasing speed.

The flat fields of Egypt lie, a ribbon of green, between cliffs that separate the Nile Valley from the desert.

V

Early Days in Egypt
Before Recorded History
(ABOUT 5000 B. C.)

In the valley of the river Nile, bathed in glittering sunshine, lay the ancient land of Egypt, a narrow strip of green in the midst of the sands of the desert.

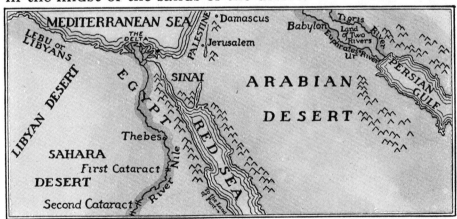

Egypt and the Nile Valley between the Sa-ha'ra and A-ra'bi-an Deserts. At its mouth, the Nile splits up into seven branches, forming a rich triangle called the Delta. It is six hundred miles from the Delta to the First Cat'a-ract and there are six cataracts from the source of the Nile to its mouth.

71

From the mountains of Central Africa, the Nile cut its way between tall cliffs that glowed rose-pink and lilac, flecked with passing shadows, and lifting clear cut outlines against a bright blue sky.

Six times the river, flowing down on its long way to the sea, halted in its course to swirl in foaming cataracts around obstructing rocks, jagged heaps of black granite, that lay as though hurled by giants across the bed of the stream.

But though there were six of these cataracts, the people who lived long ago in the valley of the Nile, had scarcely dared to venture above the first barrier of rocks.

"Go not beyond the Cataract," they said, trembling before their own fancies; "for there is the Land of Ghosts! There one may meet with a snake-headed panther, a monstrous crocodile demon or the ferocious ghost of an ape!"

An Egyptian grave of the Late Stone Age, a hole in the desert gravel surrounded by stones and heaped over with sand. The body is surrounded by jars of food, gold ornaments, flint knives and pieces of cloth.

To them the known world consisted of the blooming lands north of the Cataract, and the rich triangle of the Delta, where the Nile split up into seven branches as it emptied its waters at last in the Med'i-ter-ra'nean Sea.

For thousands of years before men knew how to write down their doings in history, they had lived there in the Nile Valley, huddled in mud-brick villages, farming a little, fishing a little, hunting gazelles and wild oxen, and burying their dead lying upright in square pits in the sand.

Painting on a prehistoric Egyptian vase showing hunters with spears and leopard-skin shields. The second warrior from the right is painted upside down, to show he has fallen, dead or wounded, to the ground. (Cairo Museum).

Each village had its own chief who led forth his handful of warriors, to fight against desert robbers or to snatch from some neighboring village a coveted bit of land; for the towns were not as yet joined by any sort of bond.

The girls made dolls of Nile mud; the boys went hunting with their fathers, the women carried pottery jars of Nile-water on their heads.

And every year in November, the Nile began to rise, fed by rains and melting snow in the mountains near its source. Unfailingly it had risen, overflowing its banks till the world

Prehistoric Egyptian warriors, from the painting at the top of the page. Note the ostrich design on the pot.

seemed a waste of waters, above which the palms and sycamores could poke up only their heads. Lotus flowers, blue
and white, floated on rippling wavelets; pelicans, storks, and
cranes stood deep in papyrus reeds on the edge of the over-
flow.

But when the Nile sank once again, it left a layer of rich
black mud, carried from Central Africa, on all the fields of
Egypt for a distance of ten miles inland, calling into teeming
life that narrow strip of rich green that wound along like a
ribbon between the tall pink cliffs.

Now over much of Egypt no rain ever fell. Skies were cloudless and brilliant blue, the earth was flooded with sunshine.
Water that dropped from the skies seemed little less than a
miracle, for water and earth to the people of Egypt were both
the gift of the Nile. Gradually the Egyptians learned how to
build ditches and little canals to carry small streams from old
Father Nile off to their distant fields or to storage reservoirs
for use when the river was low. And they raised the water up

An Egyptian shadoof as pictured upon the walls of a Nineteenth Dynasty Theban tomb. Two slaves standing
beneath the shade of sycamore trees in a garden are drawing water from a pool where lotus flowers grow.
    The shadoof was the first method used by man to raise water from the lower level of the river bed to the higher
fields, and it is still used in Egypt today. The weight on the end of the pole balances the weight of the bucket
filled with water and helps to lift it up. When the fields are quite a bit higher than the river, several relays of
shadoofs are used, each emptying into a reservoir one step higher, as shown in the upper illustration on page 71.

Toys which belonged to ancient Egyptian children. Some of the dolls had real hair and there were many mechanical toys. The baker kneading bread in the center moves up and down when the string is pulled and the lion opens and closes his mouth. Above the lion is a toy clay model of a crocodile. (From A. Bothwell Gosse.)

the steep banks of the Nile by means of tall shadoofs, upright poles with cross-beams having a bucket on one end and a large lump of mud on the other to weigh the bucket down.

What the Egyptians Thought About the World

The people living in the Nile Valley found the raising of food fairly simple, so they had plenty of leisure hours in which to take to thinking, and some began to wonder about the sun, and moon, and all the curious world.

"Who made the sun?" they asked. "And why does he leap up each morning beyond the eastern cliffs to race all day across the sky and be swallowed by the earth at night?"

But few ever answered these questions. They did not know how the world came to be, or what made the sun, moon and stars move as they seemed to do. Only the wise-men, certain that some great power must have made these things and must keep them forever in action, said after mighty pondering:

"Perhaps the sun is a god, a power that creates living things and causes them all to move; or the moon and the river Nile may be powers in themselves, other mighty gods who direct the ways of the world."

And the simple folk nodded assent, willingly letting the wise-men clear up these baffling mysteries in any way that they could.

Soon the wise-men quite forgot that they were only guessing; they said it was really true, it was perfectly certain, established fact that the sun, moon and Nile were gods!

Then they made up long tales about their gods to explain everything in the universe which they could not understand; and as the rude tribesmen sat by night about the red glow of their fires, with the stars cool and clear above them and the moon in ghostly splendor lighting the pale line of cliffs, the wise-men told their tales to a circle of open-mouthed listeners, who believed with all their simple souls, that the myths of the wise-men were true.

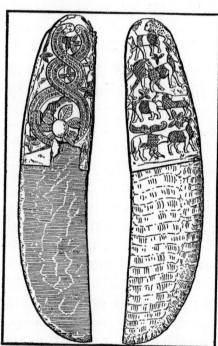

A prehistoric flint dagger with a beautiful pounded gold handle found in a desert burial pit. (Cairo Museum.)

Because the sun shone so brilliantly everywhere in Egypt and seemed to be the very power that caused all life to bloom, the people talked most of the sun-god. Some called him Re or Ra, and pictured him as a disk; others, beholding the hawk fly up and lose himself in the sun, thought that the sun was a hawk flying daily across the sky; so they called him Horus, the hawk, representing him by the sun disk with the outspread wings of a bird:

"In the beginning," the wise-men said, "there was nothing but a great watery mass which filled all space.

An Egyptian painting of the world. Nut, the goddess of the heavens, whose body is studded with stars, is supported by Shu, the god of air, while stretched out underneath is Keb, the god of the earth.

There was no earth, no sea, no sky. All at once on this watery mass, lo, there appeared an egg out of which came the sun-god.

Ra is the name of the sun-god and he is the Creator. He made himself four children—Shu and Tef'nut, Keb and Nut, who lay with him on their backs, flat on the watery mass.

In time Shu rose from the mass and, with him, his sister Tefnut. They placed their feet on Keb and, seizing Nut in their arms, they lifted her high above them.

So Keb became the earth, Nut became the sky, her body studded with stars, and Shu and Tefnut became the air which forever holds up the sky.

Then Ra made all the other gods, he made men and women, animals, plants, everything that is, and he stepped in his boat and took to travelling daily across the sky.

"That is why you see the sun leap from the east at dawn to sail all day above you and sink in the west at night."

Thus spake the solemn wise-men, but this was not their only tale about how the world was created. They peopled the earth, air, river and sky with the most fantastic spirits who

Gods of the ancient Egyptians. A-nu'bis, a jackal-headed god; Ta'urt, a hippopotamus-headed goddess. In the center, the ram-god of Thebes with the sun-disk of Ra between his horns. Above him and at the right, crude clay figures of primitive household gods. Other Egyptian gods are shown on page 11, Vol. II.

appeared, they said, as bulls or rams, as lions or crocodiles. Some of these spirits were good and some of them were bad. Some caused the crops to grow and others wrought destruction.

In time every village possessed its own guardian-spirit, its little local god, to whom the village folk prayed that they might be protected. The emblems of these gods were carried into war; and special dwellings, rude little temples, were set aside for their service.

But gradually the people, instead of being content to picture their gods as animals, gave them an animal's head and tail, with the body of a man or woman. Thus Ra became a hawk-headed man. There were lion-headed, snake-headed, hippopotamus-headed goddesses, and jackal-headed, ibis-headed, crocodile-headed gods.

And when the ordinary farmer folk, awkward and stumbling of speech, knew not with what manner of words to address their mighty gods, they turned for help to their chief who now became high-priest, and the chief set apart certain men to sing regular chants to the gods, so that these men became the priests, who passed their days in the temples.

How Writing Was Invented

Slowly ways of living began to improve in the Nile Valley. Women wove linen and made it into garments to take the place of skins. Men sought to beautify their red-brown pottery jars by painting them in black with rudely drawn figures of boats and men, or of beasts and fantastic birds. The girls had ivory combs and jewelry of ivory or bone set with beads of different colors; and here and there a young man might boast a fine stone knife with a handle of thin sheet gold in beautifully traced designs.

Within the mud-brick huts wooden couches appeared and richly carved wooden chests gaily painted in colors.

Moreover as men's possessions increased, the honest, industrious folk found need of living together, that they might protect themselves from all those savage bands that came pillaging out of the desert.

Therefore two or three villages would unite, choosing one of their chieftains as king, and repaying him for his leadership by giving him so many cattle or so many measures of grain. Thus a number of little kingdoms arose throughout the length of the Nile valley, replacing the separate towns which had each been ruled by a chief.

But, though the people of Egypt had now progressed so far, they had still discovered no way of expressing their thoughts to each other except by means of talking; for they did not know how to write.

One of the earliest ornaments found in Egypt,—a bracelet of blue stone beads, polished and strung on copper.

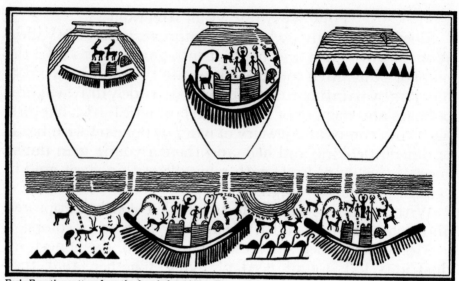

Early Egyptian pottery from the days before kings. The vases are of fine clay, polished red or black and covered with carefully drawn designs and pictures of people and animals. On the center vase a dancing woman is shown with her arms over her head. Below are pictures of antelope and ostriches and more dancing girls.

This fact now caused them much trouble. A farmer who had not wheat enough to feed his numerous family would borrow some grain from a neighbor, agreeing to return it as soon as his harvest was ripe.

But since no way had yet been devised of writing down a record of just the amount that was owing, it might be, when months had passed, that the debtor would come to repay, bearing only three measures of wheat when the neighbor had lent him four. Then the two fell to quarreling; but with nothing written down to which they could refer, there was no means of settling the question save for each to run off to the chief to plead his cause before him.

So many such disagreements arose, that men were at last obliged to work out some manner of keeping accounts, and they took to scratching rude figures on the rough mud walls of their houses,—a picture of a basket to represent a measure of grain and, after this, straight lines in a row, to count the number of measures that had been borrowed ⊍|||.

Moreover they drew pictures to record important events and thus began to develop a form of picture writing.

At first each drawing they made was a picture of the thing itself, but this was laborious work, and took too long a time when much was to be written; so they stopped making actual pictures, drawing instead simple outline-figures which they slowly came to agree should always mean the same things.

The sun was a circle with a dot in the center. ⊙ Water was three or four waves /\/\/\/\, and a star was five straight lines drawn from a common point ✶.

Then men went further still, they began to combine several drawings to indicate words of which they could make no pictures. They could not, for example, draw a picture to mean "understand."

But if they were to agree that the picture of two feet 𝄒𝄒 should always mean "stand," and the picture sign of a gate-way ⊓ should always mean "under," then by placing the two signs together ⊓ they had a simple drawing which clearly meant "understand."

When men have developed writing to such a point, signs no more depict objects but represent sounds or syllables and now can be used in such a way as to write every word

Here is a wonderful limestone statue of a scribe, in the usual position for writing. His short skirt is stretched tight by his wide-spread knees, and forms his desk. With a roll of papyrus in his left hand, his right holding the reed pen, he looks up, alert and eager, all ready to take the orders of his master.

The statue is wonderfully well-cut and so life-like that the figure almost seems to move. It was formed from a solid block of limestone by artists living about the time of the pyramid builders, and is now in the Louvre Museum in Paris.

The development of writing in Egypt from picture signs through hieroglyphics to an alphabet. The signs in the top row show that real pictures were first drawn to tell a story.

In the second row are determinatives: signs used to make clear the meanings of other signs. The first three were placed after other hieroglyphics to show that the word spelt man, god, or foreign country. The two legs in the upper right column of this row indicated motion. The picture of a plant showed that the word meant plant; the drawing of a hide indicated leather.

Below at the left, the Egyptian alphabet as it finally developed and at the right an Egyptian word and two English words written in hieroglyphics (from Breasted).

At the bottom, a line of hieroglyphics which correspond to printing in English and a line of hieratic, the rapid writing of the scribes which was like script, or handwriting in English.

Although the Egyptians developed an alphabet, it never came into common or popular use. However, in later years when Egypt conquered the eastern coast of the Mediterranean, the Phoenicians probably learned about the Egyptian alphabet and took it for their own use, changing it as seemed best to them and making the actual letters A, B, C, etc. The Ar'a-mae'an traders took this alphabet and spread it over much of the world. See Vol. II, p. 55.

that is spoken. Using drawings thus to indicate sounds is called writing by hieroglyphics and the ancient Egyptians of the Late Stone Age kept their records in hieroglyphics.

Gradually certain men came to give all their time to writing and such men were called the scribes.

As writing became more important, these scribes no longer scratched their drawings on the rough mud walls of their houses, but cut them on pieces of stone or painted them on pottery, using a clumsy blunt stick for a pen and dipping it in a kind of black ink made from vegetable gum mixed with soot.

But one day some scribe more active and eager of mind than others, discovered that the reed called papyrus which grew along the river could be split up into thin strips, which he could paste together to make a smooth tough paper.

By using a pointed reed instead of the crude blunt stick to

The Ro-set'ta Stone, now in the British Museum at London.

Although people have always known that there was once a great kingdom of ancient Egypt, the knowledge of the Egyptian language and of how to read Egyptian hieroglyphics was lost until a little more than a hundred years ago. Then it was that this famous stone, called the Ro-set'ta Stone, was discovered and from it students learned the meaning of the hieroglyphics.

The Rosetta Stone repeats in three forms of writing the same inscription which tells of certain honors which the Egyptian priests were giving a Greek king.

The top part is Egyptian hieroglyphic, the central part is Egyptian hieratic, and the bottom part is Greek.

A French student, Cham'pol'lian, had long been trying to find out the meaning of the hieroglyphics, and he had already learned what certain signs stood for by figuring out the names of Cleopatra, Ptolemy, and other well known rulers from hieroglyphic inscriptions.

Now when the Rosetta Stone was found, Champollian was able to sound out the Egyptian words by what he had already learned of hieroglyphics from well-known names of kings; and when he guessed that the Greek part of this stone said the same thing as the Egyptian, he was able to translate the Greek, and to learn what Egyptian words said the same things as the Greek.

Thus he got the meaning of many Egyptian words, from which an understanding of the whole Egyptian language was gradually worked out.

This stone is called the Rosetta Stone because it was found near the Rosetta mouth of the Nile in the Delta when the soldiers of Napoleon were digging trenches in the year, 1799.

dip in the pot of ink, he could write on this smooth yellow paper with beautiful neatness and clearness.

And when the scribes had learned how to write and count, they began to make order out of all the unrecorded days that for hundreds of thousands of years had flown by without any means of measuring.

About the year 4241 B.C. they figured out the first calendar as a means of measuring time.

As they watched the moon in the sky, they saw with what regularity it grew from a slender crescent into a full golden ball and then grew small again till it quite disappeared from the skies. So they said:

"Each time between sun risings shall be a day, each time between full moons shall be a month."

And because the rising and falling of the river Nile was the only other thing in Egypt as regular in movement as were the sun and moon, they said that the 365 days between the highest points of the Nile flood should be called a year; and they gave names to each year, calling them after some important event as the Year-of-the-Great-Flood, or the Year-of-the-Great-Fire. Henceforth by keeping a list of the year names, the scribes could tell exactly on what day, month, and year any event had occurred.

The hieroglyphics written on this jar give the name "Year of Fighting and Smiting the Northland," probably a very important date in the early days of Egypt. Year dates were kept in this manner. The jar itself is of alabaster and is now in the museum at Philadelphia.

Thus the Egyptians of the Late Stone Age discovered a system of writing and counting; they gave the world paper, pens, and ink, and figured out the first calendar.

The discovery of copper by Egyptians, exploring in the Si'nai Desert, 4,000 years before Christ, was a world event of tremendous importance. It marked the end of the fifty thousand or more years of stone weapons and tools, and the beginning of the present age of metal. At first, however, when copper was scarce, it was used for jewelry and ornaments; it was only as it became more common that spears, daggers, saws and other articles were fashioned from this new metal which could be molded and hardened in any shape desired.

But the Stone Age came to an end about 4000 years before Christ, when Egyptian adventurers, traveling afar in the sands of the Sinai Desert, found a red metal that flowed from the rock under the heat of their campfires, a glowing stream of gold easily molded when hot, but so hard when it had grown cool, that stone was broken against it.

This metal was copper and the travelers carried it back to Egypt where men soon learned that it made far better knife-blades and tools than could be made of stone.

So ended the long, weary Ages of Stone; so began better days when men went forward faster under the Age of Metal.

To the left is the King of Lower Egypt in his red crown; to the right the King of Upper Egypt in his white crown. Between are the symbols of the vulture, the bee (sometimes called a hornet), the reed, the serpent, and the hawk. The hawk wears the double crown of both Upper and Lower Egypt. The figures of the Kings are First Dynasty work found near the precious copper mines where Egyptian laborers worked on the peninsula of Sinai.

VI

The Two Lands of Egypt
The Northland and the Southland
(BEFORE 3400 B. C.)

"Give us land, more land!" came to be the constant cry of the growing Egyptian villages. Quarrels and bitter strife arose. Village fought with village to gain the coveted strips of fertile river-mud, till at last amid this confusion, the village-kingdoms vanished.

In their stead, two great kingdoms arose,—to the north was Lower Egypt, the rich green Delta of the Nile; to the south was Upper Egypt, the long narrow valley of the river, reaching from the plains of the Delta to the lands of the wild black people around the First Cataract.

In the Southland, Nekh'bet, the vulture-goddess, was worshipped, a reed was the sign of royal power, and white was the color of the land. Therefore the King of the Southland signed his official documents with a vulture or a reed; his treasury was called the White House, and he always wore a white crown, tall and bottle-shaped.

In the Northland, the serpent-goddess was worshipped,

a bee was the sign of royal power, and red was the color of the land. Therefore the King of the Northland wore a red crown, and his treasury was called the Red House.   Moreover the Bee King of the North and the Reed King of the South, each regarded himself as the great, great grandson of Ho'rus the Hawk, divinely born to rule Egypt.

With so much country under one man's rule, the kings found themselves unable to do for the people all that the village chiefs had done.   Once the kings had been soldiers and judges, overseers and priests. But, as time went on, they turned over to the nobles of their court some part of their difficult tasks.

Henceforth, one noble had charge of canals, reservoirs, and irrigation.   Another had charge of the army.   One sat as chief judge of the people.   One was collector of taxes, and one became the high-priest.

Thus each kingdom at length had a king at its head; under the king was his court, and under the court, were the people.

But even when Egypt had settled down into these two kingdoms, fighting did not cease.   Instead, each king flung himself in to the warlike task of trying to conquer the other, and so compel all of Egypt to accept his rule alone.

The fighting of this time is expressed in this slate palette of the prehistoric period. Below, lions and vultures devour the King's enemies. Above, captives are led bound before the Hawk standard.   British Museum.

Menes, the First King of All Egypt

(3407–3346 B. C.)

Now in those days, there came to the throne of the Southern Kingdom a boy of fifteen called Me'nes, the Fighter. This youth ruled with a vigorous hand over the land to the Southward; and when he had brought order there, he gathered his men together, marched down on the Delta and conquered the Northern Kingdom, making one nation at last of the two lands which had, for so long, been striving against each other.

Thus Menes became the first king to wear both the red crown of the Northland and the white crown of the Southland, to be Bee King and Reed King, Vulture King and Serpent King, and Hawk-King all in one.

A mighty hunter was Menes. In jungles along the river, he chased the elephant and the giraffe. Over the desert he hunted the lion and the fierce wild ox, with only his light bow and arrow. In little boats on the Nile he attacked the hippopotamus and the crocodile by means of harpoons and lances. Indeed, he once chased an antelope so far over the desert that he left his attendants behind and was set upon, when all alone, by his pack of half-wild dogs, who chased him with savage snarls to the edge of distant Lake Moe'ris, where he flung himself into the water and narrowly escaped the jaws of the yawning crocodiles.

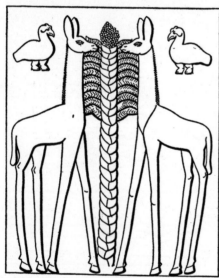

Giraffes such as Menes hunted. From a slate palette of the prehistoric period now in the British Museum.

Menes built reservoirs and storehouses where his men could keep grain and cattle paid to him as taxes; for there was no such thing as money in Egypt in those days, and workmen were paid in food.

Moreover, in order that all the men should not have to leave the fields whenever a fight arose, as they had in earlier times, Menes hired certain men always to act as soldiers with no other work to do except to protect the farms.

The King wearing the royal lion's tail and the crown of the Southland, presides at the breaking of ground for a canal. He has a hoe in his hand and a man bends toward him with a basket to take the dirt. Behind him are fanbearers. The small figures before him are standard bearers. From the mace-head of a First Dynasty King.

And when Menes had united Upper and Lower Egypt, he decided to build a new capital somewhere near the Delta; for his own old city of Thin'is, where his fathers had ruled so long, was much too far to the southward for him to govern from there the people of the Northland. So he built midway between the Two Lands, near the modern city of Cairo, a new and beautiful capital called in those days the "White Wall," but later known as Memphis.

Memphis stood near the Nile, its houses of white-washed brick, gay with painted pillars and clustered mid the greenery of tall and stately palms. The palace of Menes himself was divided into two parts, the White House for the South-

Carvings on an ebony tablet of Menes. At the left the King offers a libation to the gods; on the right a bull is caught in a temple-enclosure. Behind him a crane stands on a shrine.

land and the Red House for the Northland. Within, it was handsomely furnished. There were stools with legs carved like bulls' legs, chests of inlaid ebony, jars of fine rock crystal, and vessels of alabaster, delicate, milky white, and ground so exceedingly thin that light shone dimly through them with a gleaming rainbow lustre; for Menes was no rough king of a half-barbaric land; already civilization was two thousand years old in Egypt.

On state occasions, Menes appeared before the eyes of his people, wearing both the red crown of the Northland, and the white crown of the Southland. To his simple white linen skirt there was fastened a lion's tail as a second sign of his royal power. Before him, with stately pace, four standard bearers marched, and after him followed servants with fan-bearers and a scribe.

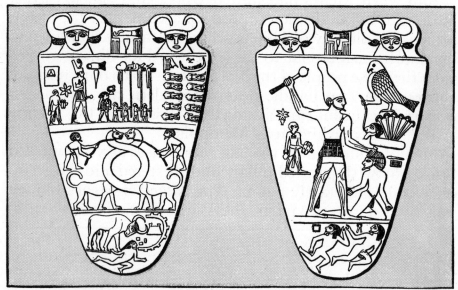

Two sides of the beautifully carved slate palette of King Narmer. At the left, below 2 heads of the cow-goddess Ha'thor, the King in the crown of Lower Egypt, walks behind 4 standard bearers and in front of his sandal-bearer. Before him are 10 headless foes with their heads between their feet. Below are 2 fantastic giraffes and a bull goring an enemy of the King. To the right the King in the crown of Upper Egypt grasps a foe by the hair, while the Hawk holds a foe by the nose, the 6 designs in the enemy's back indicating that the King slew 6,000 of the foe.

King Menes appears before his people in the crown of Upper and Lower Egypt. He is preceded by standard bearers and followed by his sandal-bearer. Drawn from the slate palette on the opposite page.

And when the people beheld their king in all his regal splendor, they thought this godlike being, great grandson of Horus the Hawk, so very high above them that they dared not breathe his name. They felt that they showed him more honor by mentioning only his palace! Therefore they called the king and his court the "Great House" which in the Egyptian language is "Per-o", or Pha'raoh, and that is how the kings of Egypt came to be called the Pharaohs.

When Menes died in process of time, he was buried in a brick-lined pit, and surrounded with fine bits of jewelry and exquisite vases and jars. His name is known to history as that of the first great King, the first law-giver and organizer to rule a united Egypt.

Pharaoh Snefru, the Betterer
(THIRD DYNASTY, ABOUT 2800 B. C.)

For centuries after Menes' time, the kings maintained with difficulty the union of the Two Lands; for the North more than once revolted, and King Narmer and other kings were obliged to smite the Northland and punish it severely to keep the two kingdoms one. It was not until Zo'ser sat on the throne, under guidance of Im'ho-tep, the famous proverb-maker, that the kingdom was at last actually firmly united.

Even in Pharaoh Snef'ru's time, 600 years after Menes, the royal palace at Memphis continued to maintain two handsome official doors, that to the South called "The Exalting of the White Crown of Snefru" and that to the North called "The Exalting of the Red Crown of Snefru," thus showing that six long centuries had not made the people forget that they had once been two lands.

The great Pharaoh Snefru, the Betterer, brought Egypt to a height of prosperity never enjoyed before. He built large vessels, some of them reaching the unheard of length of 170 feet. In these he journeyed up the Nile above the First Cataract, to punish wild Negro tribes who sometimes harried the land. And in the tenth year of his reign, he gathered together forty of his new and beautiful vessels, more ships than had ever before spread sail in a single graceful group, and he sent them out adventuring on the first expedition to foreign lands ever recorded in history.

A King of the First Dynasty dancing before the god, O-si'ris, who sits in his shrine. From an ebony tablet.

They crossed the Great Green Sea and came back laden with cedar logs from the famous forests of Lebanon, thus opening up the first trading done by way of the sea.

Moreover, Snefru sent ships to bring home copper ore from the far-off mines in Sinai, and when wandering Bed'ou-in tribes came rushing out of the hills to rob and plunder the miners, as they had been accustomed to do for generations past, Snefru fought with the robbers and punished

A King of the First Dynasty smiting a Bedouin. A relief on the rocks at Sinai, the earliest monument there. For the discovery of the copper mines in Sinai, see page 85. For the situation of Sinai, see the map, page 71.

them so severely that they dared not raid the mines again for many years to come.

Thus Snefru laid the foundations of Egypt's rule in Sinai. On the glittering white cliffs of the desert, he had two tablets erected, one of them carved with a picture showing Snefru himself smiting a Bedouin chieftain, as a warning to wandering tribesmen to leave the mines alone.

In the days of Pharaoh Snefru, order abode in Egypt, and Egypt surpassed all the nations of earth in riches and well-being, in elegance and good taste. So great indeed was King Snefru that for many years after his time, kings doing great works in Sinai said: "The like has not been done since the days of Pharaoh Snefru."

And the tellers-of-tales for centuries spun ever more marvelous stories concerning this powerful Pharaoh. One of these tales, gives a bright glimpse of life in those far-off times in Egypt.

King Snefru and the maidens. A real Egyptian folk tale, found in *Egyptian Tales* by W. M. Flinders Petrie.

Pharaoh Snefru and the Maiden Who Lost Her Jewel

It happened in the days of Pharaoh Snef'ru, that the King grew tired and weary, and he wandered through his palace seeking for pleasure to lighten his heart; but he found none.

And he said, "Haste, and bring before me the chief story teller and scribe of the rolls, Za'za-mankh."

And straightway they brought him.

And the king said, "I have sought in my palace for some delight, but I found none."

Then said Zazamankh unto Snefru, "Let thy Majesty go upon the lake of the palace, and let there be made ready a boat, with all the fairest maidens of thy palace to row thee; and the heart of thy Majesty shall be refreshed with the sight. Thou shalt see the maidens bending gracefully to the oars and thou shalt rejoice in the goodly pools of birds upon the lake. Thou shalt behold the sweet fields and the grassy shores; thus will thy heart be lightened."

Hearing, the King was delighted.

"Bring me twenty oars of ebony, inlaid with gold," he said. "Bring me twenty of the fairest maidens."

And the servants of the King obeyed him.

And the maidens rowed down-stream and up-stream, and the heart of Snefru was glad at sight of the maidens rowing.

But it chanced that one of the maidens, she who steered the boat, struck her hair with her hand, whereat her jewel of blue turquoise fell out into the water. Then the maiden stopped her song, and rowed no more; and her companions stopped and rowed no more.

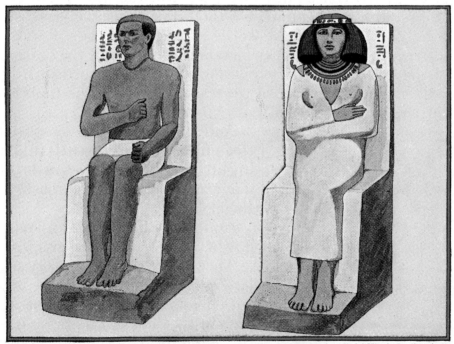

Re-ho'tep, a noble of the time of Snefru, and Nefert, his wife. This noble is called "King's Son" and was probably the son, brother, or uncle of Snefru. The statues are limestone, 4 feet high, painted in colors; the eyes are inlaid. They are the finest statues of this period ever found. Now in the Cairo Museum.

And his Majesty said: "Will you row no more?"

And the maidens replied: "Our little one, she who steereth, stops and rows no more."

Then his Majesty said to the maiden, "Wherefore rowest thou not?"

And the maiden replied, "Because of my jewel of blue turquoise which is fallen into the water."

Said Snefru unto the maiden: "Thy jewel shall be restored."

And he called for the story-teller, and they brought him Zazamankh.

And his Majesty said, "Zazamankh my brother, I have done as thou saidst, and the heart of my Majesty is refreshed with the sight of these graceful maidens. But now one of these little ones hath lost a jewel in the water, and she stops and rows no more. Do thou restore her the jewel."

So Zazamankh spake words of magic. He raised up the waters of the lake till they stood in an heap, and the bottom of the lake lay bare; he revealed the jewel in the sand; he walked into the midst of the waves, dry shod; he took up the jewel and gave it unto its mistress.

A portrait of King Snefru in colored enamel on gold from the lid of a box belonging to his wife, Queen Hetep-heres, mother of Khu'-fu. Found in her tomb at Gizeh. See page 112.

And the waves when he raised them up were twice twenty cubits high; but he spake words of magic and brought them back to their place.

And his Majesty spent a joyful day in company with the maidens.

Then rewarded he the story-teller Zazamankh.

Behold, this wonder came to pass in the days of Pharaoh Snefru, King of Upper and Lower Egypt.

The jackal-headed god of embalming, A-nu'bis, prepares the mummy of the dead. The human-headed bird is the soul of the dead holding the breath-giving sail and the scepter of power. From an old papyrus.

Life in the Land of Perfect Peace

Every year the people who lived in the valley of the Nile saw that plants which seemed brown and withered were not dead, in fact, but renewed their leaves and blossoms as soon as the Nile had refreshed them. And as the Egyptians thought of these plants, they felt within their hearts that no more did their loved ones die. They simply passed from the Nile Valley to another pleasant world where their freshness and strength were renewed. So the dreamers built up in fancy a picture of this other world which they taught to everyone else. And this is what they said:

Every morning the sun-god, Ra, glorious and glowing, rises in the East, and in his boat called "Millions of Years," begins his daily journey across the heavenly Nile, which flows in one great circle over the dome of the sky and under the depths of the earth.

In the evening Ra sinks down behind the Hills of the West and leaves his shining boat to go to the roof of the sky, where live the gods and goddesses, as well as those happy souls who have left the earth and found A'a-lu, the Land of Perfect Peace. There, from his great throne, Ra directs the universe.

To the left, rise the tall mountains of the West, beyond which on the blue zigzag waves of the underground Nile, the boat of the sun-god is just appearing. In the prow stand the goddess of Truth with a feather on her head and Hathor with the disk of the moon between her horns. To the right, an ape-demon lurks.

Life in the Land of the Perfect Peace is the same as it is in Egypt, but without its pain and sorrow. In Aalu are rich, green fields, crossed by endless canals. In Aalu grow wheat and barley, vines and fig trees and sycamores. The dweller in Aalu must plough as he did in his days on earth, only there is no famine and drought, and the work is never too heavy, but just enough to bring joy.

A dead man and his wife drink the refreshing waters of the heavenly Nile on whose banks grow palm trees as on earth. In a second picture the noble ploughs in Aalu as on earth. In later years nobles placed little statues of servants in their tombs to do the ploughing for them and relieve them of that labor in the world to come.

Some of the perils of the underworld—the human-headed serpent, devourer of souls, with the head of a soul it has eaten in each fold, and the ape-demons who fished with nets for souls. Figures from two different papyri.

Only the good ever reach that Land of Perfect Peace. Many are left in the underworld, Taut, the place of darkness, whither the spirit flees as soon as the body dies.

Every night, those who have died gather at the western mountain awaiting the boat of Ra. When the boat sinks down at sunset and Ra takes leave of it to go to his throne in the heavens, these dead folk seize the deserted barge and begin an adventurous journey down the gloom of the underground Nile toward the eastern mountain of Dawn. There are perils on every side haunting the dusk and the shadows,

The Pharaoh Ram'ses III leads his little son, who has died, into the presence of the gods. The boy still wears the side-lock of a child. From the Prince's tomb in the Valley of the Tombs of the Kings at Thebes.

and in the darkness of midnight, the boat at last comes to a halt before the Hall of Osiris, mighty Judge of the Dead.

At one end of a hall, Osiris sits on a throne of gold, amid forty-two solemn judges. I'sis, the wife of Osiris, sits by the side of her husband, and before them kneels Anubis, the jackal-headed god, with scales for weighing men's hearts.

Standing before Osiris, the soul must prove himself worthy of being sent on to Aalu; he must be able to speak, with truth, these words from the Book of the Dead:

"O ye Lords of Truth,
I have not secretly done evil against mankind;
I have not told falsehoods;
I have not made the laborer do more than his daily task;
I have not been idle;
I have not been drunk;
I have not caused hunger;
I have not murdered;
I have not stolen;
I have not cheated the weight of the balance;
I have not slandered anyone."

And when he who is waiting for judgment has maintained that he has lived in accordance with this fine standard, his heart is placed in one side of the scales of Anubis to be weighed against a feather. If the dead has been good upon earth, the scales of Anubis will balance; for the feather stands for truth, and the dead will be accepted. Entering the sun-boat again, he floats away to the eastward down the underground river until he arrives at Aalu just as the day is breaking and enters at last with joy into the Land of Peace.

Osiris, Ruler of the Underworld and Chief Judge of the Dead, was a most important god, next indeed to Ra, because upon him depended admission for every man to the Land of Perfect Peace. Whenever a man died in Egypt, the people said of him: "Our friend has gone to Osiris."

The heart of the dead in a jar is weighed by the jackal-headed A-nu'bis against the feather of truth. The ibis-headed Thoth waits to record the verdict and behind him the gruesome monster A'mem-it, eater of souls, crocodile, lion and hippopotamus combined, stands ready to eat the heart if the scales do not balance. At the left the man and his wife await the verdict. Above sit the judges before whom the two have just made confession of righteousness. (From an old papyrus). The Book of the Dead arose gradually between the Pyramid Age and the Middle Kingdom, but charms and texts included in that book appear from very early times written on the inside of coffins.

The Story of Osiris and Isis

The sun behind the sand hills was setting gold and crimson, when a tall man, broad and strong, and a woman with glowing hair, stopped beside a rude temple, close to the Nile in Thebes.

As the waters of the river flamed into sudden fire, the man and the woman lifted their hands, bowed three times to the earth, and sang a short hymn to Ra.

Then the man sat down on a stone, took a reed pipe from his belt and softly played sweet music, while the woman sang to his piping in a voice that was rich and tender.

Scarcely had the last sweet strains died away on the air, when an ancient man in a long white robe, came slowly toward the wayfarers.

"A pleasant evening unto you both," he said.

"And unto thee, O my father," replied the man. "Canst tell us where in this city, travellers may find lodging?"

The old man said not a word; but he gazed upon the new-

comers with steady, questioning eyes. Then he bowed his head with reverence and kissed the ground before them.

"I am priest of this temple," he said. "Long have I known of your coming through the truth that is writ in the stars. Lodge in my humble home, for all that I have is yours."

"Sobeit, faithful one," said the man, "but I charge thee straitly, tell no one, whence we came or why."

The ancient one bowed to the dust, while the man took his wife by the hand and led her away to the temple.

In this manner did Osiris and Isis come to the land of Egypt. Thereafter, each day saw the two somewhere among the people, advising, helping, cheering. Wherever they were most needed, there they seemed to be. No hand so cooling to the fevered brow as that of Isis, the merciful; no voice so soothing to the children. And Osiris was busy among the men working in the fields, showing them how to make a plow, how to lift the water up the steep banks of the Nile, how to lighten their burdens.

Soon the King of Thebes, hearing news concerning the

stranger, summoned Osiris before him. And Osiris found grace in his eyes and the King spake thus to Osiris:

"I have heard much of thy skill and it pleaseth me to bid thee teach the men of my court."

So Osiris thereafter came daily to teach the men of Thebes. And when the king passed to Aalu, leaving no heir to the throne, the people turned to Osiris and made him King of Thebes.

Then Osiris gathered together a worthy band of followers and journeyed up and down the valley of the Nile, teaching all who would listen. Therefore it came to pass that many little kingdoms, drawn by his wisdom and goodness, begged him to rule them also, and he became King of all Egypt.

Years of happiness followed, years of peace and plenty until a certain dark day when one came to Osiris and said: "Set, thy brother is here, son of thy father, Keb, the earth; son of thy mother, Nut, the heavens; and grandson of thy grandsire, Ra, the Lord of the Sun."

So Osiris welcomed his brother and gave him princely chambers within the royal palace; but Set was lord of evil,

short, deformed and ugly, and from the time of his coming, peace departed from Egypt. Restlessness came with grumbling, quarreling, and discontent. Secretly, Set was plotting, full of envy and hate. Osiris, the well beloved, shedding joy in the land, Osiris should be slain—Egypt should fall to Set,—Set should be king of the land.

So Set laid plans for a feast, bidding Osiris come with all the men of his court. But the heart of Isis was sad, heavy with dark foreboding, because of the love she bore unto Osiris, her lord. And she said: "My husband, I beg thee, go not unto this feast. My heart is dwelling with shadows. Danger threatens thy head."

But Osiris put her aside and answered her gently thus: "Fear not, O my beloved. He unto whom I go is son of my father and mother, brother unto me."

And he went to the chambers of Set, to the chambers of flowers and music. And lo, in the midst of an hall stood a great metal box with carvings, a box of such delicate workmanship that all who beheld it marvelled.

Then Set gave his crooked leer, "Lie down in the box!" he cried in the ears of all his guests. "Whoever finds it to fit him shall have the box for his own."

And the guests made haste to obey, for each desired the treasure; but some were too tall and some were too short. Only Osiris, stretching himself at full length in the chest, found it a perfect fit; but when he lay helpless within it, Set gave a sudden cry: "The box is yours forever!"

He slammed down the lid, shot the bolts into place, and called his men to pour through the cracks a stream of molten lead.

They placed the box on a boat; they rowed it out to midstream; they flung it into the Nile!

A sudden flame leapt up. Then all was darkness and

silence. Osiris was slain, was slain,—the victim of brotherly hate. Osiris, was slain, was slain!

Through the long night Isis waited, but when she beheld the flame leaping up from the river, she knew that the worst was come,—Osiris, her lord, was dead!

Soon came the noise of battle,—Set's men taking the city! Shouts, harsh cries and clamor,—Set's men taking the palace, Set himself at the door crying:

"Isis shall marry Set! Open to Set, thine husband!"

But the heart of Isis was heavy; and she changed herself into a swallow and flitted away through the window, even at that very moment when Set burst in at the door.

Scarce knowing which way to turn, Isis flew off down the river,—off toward the distant Delta, ever seeking Osiris, now guided by an old woman, and now by a bevy of children, and comforted at last by fairy voices who sang:

> "Lady so beautiful, he, thy beloved,
> Lies no more here where the Nile seeks the sea;
> Leave these sad marshes and seek for him further,
> Seek mid the limbs of the tamarisk tree."

Then came the strange folk of the swamps and said: "Thy box was carried far out to sea and cast up at distant Byb′los, beyond the forests of Lebanon, where it lodged within the branches of a spreading tamarisk tree. The King of Byblos cut down the tree for a pillar to hold up his palace; but the box is still hidden within it."

So Isis made off to Byblos, and hired herself out as nurse-maid to nurse the King's son back to health after a serious illness. And she begged in return for what she had done, that she might be given the box that was hid in the tamarisk tree.

Returned again to the marsh country, Isis broke open the chest and removed the form of her husband, kneeling

beside it with outstretched arms and chanting a hymn to Ra.

Then lo, in the west a wonder! The sun-god's boat which had sunk for the night appeared again on the hill, a glorious disc of gold, and in it stood Ra himself with his face toward the two on the sand.

A flame overspread the heavens and bathed the earth in fire. With a crash, the boat suddenly vanished, and darkness covered the world; but Osiris had come to life; and when the stars came out and the moon shone a silver crescent reflected in the river, two figures sat side by side in the sand, clasping each other's hands.

Thereafter Osiris and Isis lived in the marshes of the Delta, dwelling in a little hut made of woven rushes.

And there the babe Horus was born to make their joy complete. In the cool of the evening they sat by the hut, Osiris playing his pipe and Isis singing lullabies to the babe that lay in her lap. Sometimes they sailed on the river, moved by the gentle breezes, and thus the days and years slipped by while the child grew in beauty and strength.

But Set had never given up searching the land for Isis; so one day he came on Osiris chasing a fleet gazelle and he ordered his men to kill him. This time they not only slew him, but cut his body in fourteen pieces and buried each piece in a different place, that Isis might never again succeed in bringing her husband to life!

Isis must needs hide her son in the midst of a floating island, and once more set out wandering on the weary search for her lord.

And now Ra came to her aid. He sent her the ibis-headed Thoth, wisest of all the gods, to guide her steps in searching.

Thus the faithful wife gathered from all the four corners of Egypt the body of Osiris. And at each spot where a part was found, there a temple was built. At A-by'dos, where she came on his head, rose the finest temple of all. And Anubis, the jackal-headed god, helped her prepare the pieces; magic words were spoken, and Osiris once again rose and moved and breathed the breath of life.

King Tut-ankh-amen as Horus the Avenger. A beautiful golden statuette found in his tomb. Cairo Museum.

But now Osiris could dwell no longer upon the earth. Because he had twice passed through the gates of that which men called death, Ra sent him down to the Underworld to be the Judge of the Dead; and Isis went back to the island, hid in the marshes of the Delta, to bring up Horus, her son, in the memory of his father, his goodness and his suffering.

And Horus grew up, a faithful son, and when he was come to manhood, he said: "I will go and fight this Set! I will go and avenge my father!"

And Ra in those days heard complaints from all the people of Egypt because of the hard rule of Set. So he took the form of a man and went unto Horus and said: "Together we will fight Set."

Then Horus took the form of an hawk, and flew up high in the sky to look over all the land, and in the marshes far to the north, he spied the armies of Set making ready for battle.

Together, he and his great grandsire, Ra, sailed off down the river, gathering an host as they went; but evil creatures who favored Set placed themselves in their way, demons who made themselves crocodiles or raging hippopotami to fight against the two heroes; and when these were overcome, there followed a mighty battle with all the forces of

Set, a battle which raged day after day throughout the whole length of the land.

Terrible was the conflict. Set rushed forth, ugly and powerful, driving all before him. For two days no man knew on which side the victory would be. But when the third day dawned, the foes came face to face.

"At last, thou murderer," Horus cried, "behold thy day of reckoning!"

"At last, thou son of my hate," roared Set, "behold how I shall slay thee!"

Blows rained like storms with thunder. The two armies stopped their fighting and turned to watch the combat.

This way and that the rivals reeled, till at last the long spear of Horus, gleaming with lightning flash, sped to the heart of Set. The evil one fell with a groan; earth shook and the soldiers of Horus shouted aloud in their joy: "Set is dead; he is dead! The Lord of evil is dead! He will trouble the world no more!"

And Horus the Hawk, reigned in Egypt, and his son, and his son's son followed him; and all the kings of Egypt are descendants of Horus the Hawk.

King Khufu, his Queen and 2 children watch the building of the Great Pyramid of Gizeh in the desert near Memphis. The little girl is surprisingly yellow-haired. See upper picture, page 114. The little boy Men-keu-re' was later Pharaoh and built the third Pyramid. (See page 120.) Hidden away in the center of this great pyramid was the secret inner chamber where Khufu hoped his body would rest undisturbed by robbers. His hope was in vain however; for his pyramid was ransacked and his body had disappeared when modern explorers found the chamber.

VII

The Pyramid Builders

The Great Pyramid of Khu'fu (Che'ops) at Gizeh

(FOURTH DYNASTY, ABOUT 2789–2767 B. C.)

Life after death, the Egyptians believed, depended on preserving the body of the dead. If the dead man's body were destroyed, his life in the world to come, would be destroyed. Therefore they always embalmed their bodies, soaking them in oils, treating them with spices, and afterwards wrapping them round with strips of linen cloth to keep the air away.

The mummy, thus embalmed, was placed in a wooden case brightly painted in colors; and when it was laid in the tomb, it was furnished with food and clothing, and whatever it

Stages in the development of the pyramid. From the square stone "mastabas" on the left, through the first piling of one mastaba on another, to the real "step" pyramid of Pharaoh Zoser. For prehistoric pit tombs see page 72.

might be expected to need in the world to which it had gone.

At first, in the earliest times, the mummies were taken to the desert to be buried in brick-lined pits; but a certain Pharaoh, seeking to leave a monument more glorious than a simple heap in the desert, ordered that over his grave should be built a rectangular structure, made of square-hewn stones.

This structure was called a mas'ta-ba, and it served as a model for tombs until the Pharaoh Zoser, piling up rows of mastabas, each smaller than the one below, made the famous step-pyramid which can still be seen at Sak-ka'ra, the first large structure of stone ever made in the world.

A doorway in the tomb of Pharaoh Zoser ornamented with glazed blue and white tiles in a beautiful pattern. This is the first known use of glazed tiles, but the perfection of the workmanship shows that glazing had already been long in use. The arch is unusual in Egyptian architecture, though widely used in Babylon and Assyria. Note the prints of naked feet on the floor. Were they made by builder, priest or visitor? No one knows.

Pharaoh Snefru improved on Zoser's work by filling in the steps; and after Snefru came Khu'fu, who built the Great Pyramid at Gi'zeh, the largest pyramid of all.

King Khufu, "the Energetic," son of Pharaoh Snefru and Hetep-heres, his queen, was a powerful, ambitious man. He felt within himself a mighty urge to act, to organize, and direct. He dreamed of erecting at Gizeh, behind the city of Memphis, the largest pyramid ever made, Ik-hut', the Glorious Place, a structure so gigantic that men should see it for miles around, a monument for all time to the glory of his race.

A hundred thousand men King Khufu gathered together, an army of laborers dwelling in huts out on the edge of the desert, and they worked to the chanting of building songs and the crack of the overseer's whip.

Two million, three hundred thousand stones, each weighing two tons and a half, must be dragged up into place! And since no derrick was known to lift the heavy stones, the workmen made sloping hills of brick to lean against the structure as the building gradually rose, and up these they hauled the stones even to the very top.

Queen Hetep-heres, mother of Khufu, in her carrying chair of wood encased in gold. This chair, 5000 years old, was recently discovered in the Queen's tomb by Dr. George Reisner, Director of the joint expedition of Boston Museum and Harvard University. Khufu loved his mother dearly and when her tomb at Da-shur' was robbed, he had her sarcophagus reburied with all the care of a loving son, secretly placing it near his own pyramid at Gizeh.

Twelve hundred blocks laid each day, some thirty men dragging each block, wetting the runners of their sledges to make them slip with ease,—that was the sight men saw daily in the busy bee-hive at Gizeh!

Thirteen acres of ground covered solid with stone and towering up to a height of 481 feet! And Khufu, the Energetic, organizing it all, and seeing it carried through.

Some of King Khufu's sons were old enough to serve him by taking charge of the quarries, but some such as little Menkeure, who would one day sit like his father upon the throne of Egypt, were still so young as to do no more than gaze in round-eyed wonder at the pyramid rising before them, a miracle of white stone.

In spite of his forceful nature, Khufu, the pyramid-builder, was a man of warm affections. He loved his mother, Hetep-heres, he loved his wife, the slim Queen Mertitefs, lady of the wondering eyes, and all his big brood of lively children, one of whom, a little girl, ran about the palace, surprisingly yellow-haired amid the dark locks of Egypt.

Sometimes, to amuse his family, Khufu summoned clever magicians to perform their tricks at his court, even ordering his servants to pay one skilful wizard a thousand loaves each day with a hundred jugs of beer, an ox, and a hundred bunches of onions!

Around the base of his pyramid, smaller pyramids rose for other members of his family, and beyond these lay tombs of the nobles, constructed in orderly rows.

Two figures of Queen Mertitefs, wife of Khufu, the lady of the wondering eyes. (From the Leyden Museum)

At the left Hetep-heres II, the yellow-haired daughter of Khufu. Next, her daughter and her daughter's children. From the tomb of the daughter, Queen Meresankh.

These tombs were painted on the inner walls with gay scenes of ploughing and reaping, feasting, hunting, fishing, and all that made the life of the noble busy and happy on earth.

Important men, indeed, were Pharaoh Khufu's nobles; for in days of famine the smaller land-owners had sold their fields in return for food, and now served the nobles as slaves. Thus Khufu's nobles were lords of much land, surrounded by many servants.

They dwelt in light, airy houses built of wood and brick, their living rooms opened on every side, with gay-colored hangings to close them in case of sand-storms or wind.

They drank from beautiful cups shaped like the lotus-lily; they ate from spoons with handles that blossomed into flowers; they lay on couches of ebony, inlaid with

Anklets of Khufu's mother, Queen Hetep-heres I, graduated to fit the legs and beautifully inlaid with the figure of a dragonfly in green malachite, blue lapis-lazuli and red carnelian. From Hetep-heres' tomb.

ivory and gold; they sat on stools finely carved, having legs like the legs of a beast, with the cloven hoof of an ox or a lion's claw for feet. They stared up at ceilings painted blue, dotted with sun, moon and stars, and resting, like the sky itself, on graceful pillars of palm trees; they trod on floors painted green with birds on the swaying grasses and fish gliding in and out. Indeed, every object they used was gay with vivid color and beautiful in design.

A family of the Old Kingdom enjoying themselves in the garden. The toys of the children, the dancers, musicians, and frieze of geese, are all copied from real articles and paintings found in tombs of the period. See Toys, page 75. The Egyptians were the first people to make pillars and to beautify the things they used. (See page 191.)

And these elegant nobles of Khufu's held their heads very high, for they were handsome fellows. Their skins were light reddish brown, their faces and heads were close-shaven; but they wore, when fully dressed, elaborate wigs of wool and square artificial beards attached to their ears by a string. Their spotless, white, linen kilts reached only as far as the knees, while the upper part of their bodies was bare, save for a wide enameled collar, set with precious stones.

Thus garbed, they received their visitors or made the rounds of their great estates, inspecting the farms and villages; for they were peaceful fellows, having no wish to fight, but dearly loving their fields, chiefly concerned with farming and building their splendid tombs.

A noble of the Old Kingdom carved on wood, Cairo Museum. The bust of a woman, a masterpiece of this period, Carnarvon Collection. Note her wig which does not entirely cover her hair in front. Children of the Old Kingdom playing leap-frog. From the collection of the Haskell Museum, Oriental Institute, University of Chicago.

The wives and daughters of the nobles wore close-fitting white linen garments, reaching from the breast to the ankles, their legs bound in so tightly that they could scarcely walk. Beside them the children ran gaily, wearing no clothing at all.

In the gardens of their fine villas, these people passed their spare time. By the side of a limpid pool in which darted gay-colored fish, they sat beneath the trees, absorbed in some interesting game, listening to tinkling music, or watching the dancing-women posing in slow-moving dances, while the children played nearby, romping with a pet monkey, nursing a jointed doll or laughing at the antics of some comical jumping jack.

Sometimes the noble and his wife got into a frail little boat, its prow and stem shaped like a flower, and floated out on the marshes amid the tall reeds and rushes, the lady plucking lotus flowers while the noble hunted wild fowl.

Often the Lord of the Manor took one of his sons as companion, and went to inspect his farms. In Spring, he pointed out to the boy yokes of oxen ploughing, with men and women scattering seed, and flocks of donkeys or goats driven over the fields to push the seed into the ground. In autumn, he showed him men cutting grain or threshing with patient oxen, driving the great beasts over the stalks to press out the heads of the wheat and singing as they drove:

"O thresh the corn, ye oxen,
Come, tread the grain out faster;
The straw is yours for eating,
The grain is for your master."

In the villages father and son looked in on coppersmiths' shops, on goldsmiths, jewelers, carpenters, joiners, ship-

A noble hunting with a boomerang, his boat about to glide into a clump of papyrus reeds alive with birds. Some of these birds feed the young in their nests, others sit upon eggs, while a weasel sneaks up to steal eggs. Above, birds and butterflies flit about. Below are fish in the water with a hippopotamus and crocodile. The artificial beard of the noble is fastened to his chin by strings, a typical fashion in Egypt where men were clean shaven. In later days it was only the Pharaoh and statues of the gods to whom custom permitted a beard.

builders, weavers; they stopped before those who made colored glass of sand mixed with limestone and ash; they watched the potter turn his wheel, a small round platform of wood whereon the clay went spinning while the potter skilfully pressed it, till he fashioned it into shape.

In the market places they saw men exchanging things in barter, a fan for a bundle of onions, a wooden box for a fish, or gold and copper rings as the price of merchandise.

And out on the Nile before them, the river was alive. There were barges laden with produce being carried to distant markets or to one of the King's store-houses, while pleasure craft darted among them with bright-colored awnings and sails, the oarsmen singing a rowing song as they swept away down the stream.

Such was life in Egypt in the days of the Pyramid Builders, an age of simple elegance, of youthful freshness and strength.

A scene of bartering under the Old Kingdom before the days of money. In the upper left square a fish dealer sits before his rush basket cleaning a fish. A woman offers him a wooden box in exchange. Behind her another woman offers earthen jars for a box of ointment. In the upper right square a man offers a collarette for a white cake, but the seller says that is not enough, so the buyer says: "Then take the sandals as well."

In the lower left square, a woman offers a wooden box for a string of beads and a man offers fish-hooks which the tradesman is refusing. In the lower right square a man offers a bead necklace for a bunch of onions, while behind another man waits to buy his onions with a fan. From a tomb painting at Sakkara.

The pyramids and the Sphinx as they are today. At the right is the Great Pyramid. In the middle is the Second Pyramid which looks taller than the first because it stands on higher ground. Between the paws of the Sphinx is an altar. The face of the Sphinx was once painted red, its eyes black, its head-dress white.

The Lesser Pyramids and the Sphinx

Now the Pharaohs who came after Khufu also built great pyramids to keep their bodies safe. Khaf're, the son of Khufu, came to the throne while his stepmother, Queen Mertitefs, Khufu's widow was still in the Land of the Living, and he made the old lady Mistress of the Royal Wardrobe and Superintendent of the Chamber of Wigs and Head-dresses unto the King! Moreover, he married the daughter of Khufu, and carried on Khufu's stern, severe, efficient, vigorous rule.

A man of unconscious dignity, aloof and unapproachable, Khafre looked out on the world with the untroubled gaze of one whose will has never been opposed.

Pharaoh Khafre, builder of the Second Pyramid, dignified, efficient, powerful, unapproachable and aloof.

Near the Great Pyramid of Egypt, Khafre built a second pyramid, smaller than the first, but standing on higher ground so it seemed to be even larger, and gleaming with delicate pink all about the base, being bordered with fine pink granite quarried far up the Nile.

Then he ordered his sculptors to carve from a limestone hill a huge, overpowering figure, 70 feet high and 150 feet long, with the body of a lion and the face of Khafre himself, a wise smile parting his lips, his eyes far-away and dreamy.

This creature was the Sphinx. Its face was painted red, its eyes were black and its headdress, white. The forepaws, 50 feet long, were stretched out in front of the body and between them lay an altar.

Stark and splendid rose the Sphinx, crouching on the desert,—the embodiment of the spirit of those ancient pyramid-builders, keeping guard over Egypt.

Pharaoh Menkeure, builder of the Third Pyramid, jolly and good-natured. All his statues show this smile.

Now after Khafre's death there came to the throne of Egypt, Men-keu-re', son of Khufu, who had been no more than a child at the time of his father's death. Menkeure was a merry fellow, with mirthful eyes and a face ever ready to blossom forth into

smiles. Not for him the stern rule, the ruthless, hard effi-
ciency of Khufu and of Khafre. He neither could nor would
drive his people to labor or wring from them heavy taxes
to build himself a tomb. He was mild, sweet-tempered,
joyous, easy-going, and laughter-loving. Under him strong
discipline ceased. The Pharaohs no more ruled Egypt with
a heavy rod of iron.

And Menkeure built the third pyramid; but he neither
made it as fine nor half as large as the other two; yet he
placed his small unpretentious tomb beside those two magnificent ones as though defying the contrast, perhaps with
an inward smile as one who would say: "Behold, to run a
race seeing who can heap up to his memory the biggest pile
of stone, is not the aim of life. I have been happy and
merry. With that I am content!"

Thus the pyramids and the Sphinx stand on the sands
of the desert while ages come and go, the most enduring
monument to the ancient glory of Egypt and the vast,
creative energy of the Pharaohs of the Old Kingdom, who
ruled with such vigor and power that two thousand years
after their time they were worshipped as gods in Egypt.

Around this third pyramid likewise clung legends of Queen Nitokris, whose spirit was said to haunt the place. It
was concerning Queen Ni-to'kris, called Rho-do'pis or Rosy-Cheeked in the Greek, that the first *Cinderella* stories arose.
    According to an ancient Egyptian folk-tale, Nitokris was bathing in the Nile when an eagle flew off with one
of her sandals, which he carried to Memphis and dropped in the lap of the King who sat administering justice. So
deeply was the King moved with admiration for the sandal that he declared he would wed none but the owner
of it. And he sent his Chief Scribe through the land with the sandal borne on a cushion before him.
    The scribe tried the sandal on lady after lady, until at last he found Nitokris and brought her to the King
to be his wife and Queen. This story is outlined in Maspero's *Dawn of Civilization*, Ebers' *Introduction to an
Egyptian Princess*, Lang's *Introduction to Grimm's Fairy Tales*, and by the Greek Strabo and the Roman, Aelian.

The island of Elephantine near the First Cataract, looking across to the Negro huts of the Aswan or market.

Harkhuf (Har-koof'), The First Great Explorer

(SIXTH DYNASTY, ABOUT 2500 B. C.)

For centuries the huge piles of black granite rock around which the Nile went rushing in the rapids of the First Cataract, were the end of the world for the people of Egypt. Boats could not pass that point, and in the region round about dwelt the turbulent tribes of black men, fierce, barbaric savages, the "people-with-the-crinkly-hair."

And yet it was from these black men of Nubia and Kush, that the Egyptians got ivory and ebony, panther and leopard skins, ostrich feathers and gold, as well as miserable trains of unfortunate Negro slaves. Therefore exploring the Southland became the great work of the Pharaohs and nobles from the time of Pep'i I.

The nobles who went to Nubia were bold, adventurous fellows. They came of a family called the Elephantine lords because they used the elephant as their sign and lived on an island named Iebo, "the city of the Elephant."

These lords likewise had the title: "Keepers of the Door of the South," and it was their duty to protect the border-land at the foot of the First Cataract, so that Negro tribes could not swarm down and enter by force into Egypt.

In the days of Pepi I, they had already made this district so safe, that when Pepi dispatched one, U'ni, to bring him back fine granite from the quarries near the Cataract, Uni was able to take out the stone amid the savage tribes with the help of "only one warship," a hitherto unknown feat.

The City of the Elephant, gay with painted pillars, stood among the jagged black rocks below the First Cataract.

On the Eastern mainland opposite, rose the huts of the Aswan or market where Negroes coming down from the upper banks of the river exchanged their goods with Egyptians who rowed across from the city.

Hundreds of fierce barbarians swarmed about that market,—wild and warlike Ma'zoi bearing bows and clubs, powerful Wa'wats and Seth'us with feathers in their hair.

Graphic scenes from Egyptian tombs. At the extreme right is a Negro driver of a giraffe with a monkey climbing its neck. Following him are three men (from another tomb) bearing sticks of ebony and an ivory tusk. The first of these leads a live leopard, while the second and third carry beautiful skins; the third also leads a baboon.

These were the tribes who lived as far south as Egyptian knowledge went; but who lived further south still? That was the interesting question. There all was strange and mysterious; fancy made up for knowledge; there in that hazy south was the terrible Land of Ghosts.

Now when the boy-King Mer-en-ra' sat on the throne of Egypt, a certain stout-hearted young prince, Har-khuf' of Elephantine, made up his mind to push further south than any had gone before. He had already made one journey as far as the Land of Yam to lay out for the young Pharaoh a highway across the desert, but then his father went with him, as he was considered too young to manage the party alone. On his second trip however, his father remained at home. Harkhuf set out alone, heading his own caravan.

A Negro woman and her babies from the tomb of Huy at Thebes. The hair of the babies has been gathered in bunches just as Negro pickaninnies love to have it done today. The skirts of the woman are gaudy with stripes in brilliant colors, scarlet, blue and yellow.

Leaving the little reedy bay opposite Elephantine, he climbed a rocky hill whence he looked back and saw the beautiful Island-city gleaming like a jewel on the bright blue waters below. To the north-ward stretched away the road to Lower Egypt; to the west, across the sands, rose those lonely western hills over which flitted the ghosts.

Resolutely Harkhuf turned his back on the Island-city and descended into the desert, ablaze in a blinding sun.

On and on he journeyed over the endless sand-waves that lay like a sea before him.

Monsters Harkhuf's men feared to meet in the desert. The serpent-headed lion, the griffin and hawk-headed Sag are from tombs at Beni Hasan, to whose owners they were so real that they were painted among the actual beasts of the desert, seen by the nobles when hunting. The fourth monster is from the Book of the Dead. (See page 100.)

Past the lofty mountains of Wa'wat he went, past the rocks of Seth'u and the shining green bay of Irth'et, till he came to the land of the Ma'zoi.

And now he had reached the very end of the known world of his day. Henceforth he was forging forward into the Vast Unknown. His men, as they marched by day over the shining sands or sent their campfires at night, flaming against the sky, expected at any moment to meet a monster or bogey, more to be dreaded, by far, than the fiercest black Negro chieftain. They might catch a glimpse of the Sag, a lioness with the head of a hawk and a tail like a lotus-flower! Or they might see that hideous creature, the crocodile-hippopotamus, who lurked in the Underworld to snatch the hearts of the dead!

In every mysterious shadow they saw a pursuing ghost.

To their great surprise, however, they never encountered the Sag nor caught so much as a glimpse of one little ghost or specter. Neither on this desert road did they fall in with many bands of savage Negro tribesmen. The black men stayed by the river, in the narrow strips of green.

And so Harkhuf and his men came safely at last to Yam, a land of wonderful loveliness with shady groves of tamarisk and rosy hills of sandstone gazing at their reflections standing upside down in the Nile.

Harkhuf then gathered together gifts in very great quantities, panther-skins, ivory, ebony, precious incense, and gold.

But when he set out from Yam to return again to Egypt, he boldly refused to go by the round-about path through the desert. Instead he went down the river-road, a route that had never been taken before by official or caravan-master, out of fear of the wild Negro chieftains.

Straight through the land of the blacks he went, where their squalid little mud huts clustered together in villages. Men, women and round-eyed children gazed at him, wondering or threatening, but not one dared to attack him.

And so at the end of eight months he returned in safety to Elephantine.

Henceforth he spent all his days and nights with his caravan, he wrote, ever carrying out with zeal what his lord desired and commanded. And thus, in process of time, he set out for a third time to go to the land to southward.

He journeyed long and he journeyed far till he came to the borders of Yam; but when he caught sight of the stately palms that make the oasis, Kur'kur, an isle of green in the desert, he beheld the Chieftain of Yam in all his barbaric splendor, setting forth in battle array to smite a tribe of Libyans, white-skinned, tattooed rascals, cousins of those rude pale-faces who dwelt across the Great Green Sea in the unknown lands of Europe.

Fierce was the Negro Chieftain and fierce were his intentions. His head-dress bristled with anger. He had quarreled with those white-skinned Libyans, and he meant, he declared with force, to knock them off the earth, "as far as the western corner post of the canopy of heaven!"

But Harkhuf had other purposes for which to use the Chieftain. So he followed the angry savage and smoothed down his ruffled feathers, till he praised all the gods for the sake of Pharaoh, and made peace with his foes. Then Harkhuf invited the Chieftain to act as his escort to Yam, and the

The angry Negro chieftain threatens the white-faced Libyan chief while Harkhuf makes peace between them. The Negroes of the upper Nile and the Libyans who lived on the oases of the Libyan Desert west of Egypt were from the earliest times the chief enemies of Egypt. The Libyans were white-faced barbarians dressing their hair in this peculiar style with bangs and one strand over the shoulder. They were most elaborately tattooed, sometimes with whole scenes of the chase, and wore ostrich feathers in their hair while the Negroes wore stiff quills. In these days the white races were the barbarians; the red Mediterranean races, Egyptians and Cretans, were the cultured people.

raging Chief of the Crinkly-Hair turned about like a lamb and attended the bold explorer back to the innermost parts of his own little-visited land. He even agreed, indeed, to send a band of his warriors to act as a guard to Harkhuf when he should return to Egypt.

Thus Harkhuf was able to take back from this expedition more rich produce of Yam than he had ever dared try to bring home with him before.

He loaded 300 asses with incense, ebony, grain, panther-skins and ivory, and set out from Yam by the river-road, so surrounded by great black warriors that even with this rich load which would have made splendid plunder, he dared face the dreaded Chieftain of Irthet, Sethu and Wawat who lived on the banks of the river.

When that famous Chieftain of Irthet beheld Harkhuf's fierce guard; when he looked on those tall black warriors, and saw how strong and numerous were the men of Egypt with him, he was awed and overcome; for he realized that Harkhuf was more important and resolute than any noble or caravan-master who had ever before gone to Yam; and he made no effort to plunder his richly laden train; but brought him a present of bulls and small cattle and escorted him on his way homeward across the desert highlands.

In time Harkhuf reached the Nile, where he saw a stately ship with a party sent out by Pharaoh under his Master of the Bath to bring the returning adventurers date-wine and cakes with bread and beer, in case they had run short of food on their long and dangerous journey.

This ship bore Harkhuf in safety back to Elephantine, where he rested from his labors in the coolness of his garden, telling long tales of Yam.

Now by the command of Mer-en-ra', Uni, the older adventurer and servant of Pepi I, had built a series of five canals around the First Cataract, so that boats could go

further southward. His work and that of Harkhuf so deeply impressed the black men that it was now thought wise to have the young King, Merenra, go in state to A-swan', the very first Pharaoh of Egypt ever to go so far southward.

Accordingly in January, the coolest time of year to visit those sun-bathed regions, Merenra set out, splendidly dressed and attended. On the eastern bank of the Nile, within sound of the First Cataract, the Negro chieftains gathered in all their finest feathers, to see this young "Son of the Sun-god," this boy-King in all his glory. And so deeply were they impressed by the overpowering splendor with which the boy was attended, that two inscriptions were cut on the rocks to record the important event:

"The coming of the King himself, standing behind the hill-country, while the chiefs of Mazoi, Irthet and Wawat did obeisance and gave great praise."

But this triumphant reception, proclaiming the extension of Egypt's power to the southward, was the last public act of the young Merenra; for on his return to Memphis he died, and his half-brother Pepi the Second, a child of only six, was placed on the throne in his stead, to wear the heavy crowns of Upper and Lower Egypt, and be addressed with all the impressive, high-sounding titles of Pharaoh.

Now Harkhuf, at this time, was far out in the desert, making a fourth trip to Yam. And when he heard that Pepi was come to the throne in Egypt, he determined to search out for him a little dancing pigmy. Surely such a gift would please the heart of a child!

So Harkhuf pushed further southward than he had ever gone before, searching for a pigmy. At last he found what he wanted, a lively little black dwarf dancing before the figure of his crude, fantastic god, posing, twirling, stepping, in the maze of the sacred dance.

Placing the little man in the midst of his caravan, Harkhuf returned to Elephantine, where he had to leave his asses and go by ship to Memphis. And from Elephantine he sent messengers to tell the little king what he was bringing home. "Never before," he wrote the boy, "has a pigmy like him been brought home by anyone who has reached Yam."

Statue of a dwarf of the Old Kingdom. Cairo Museum. See page 213.

The child was beside himself, wild with excitement and joy. A dwarf, a real live pigmy, such as no one had seen in Egypt in his day! He could hardly wait for his coming. For all his covering over of crowns and royal names, the little Pharaoh of Egypt was very much a child. Indeed, so anxious was he to see the pigmy alive, that he called a scribe to assist him and with all the labored struggles of any child of six, he wrote Harkhuf a letter to bid him have trustworthy servants watch

the precious creature every single moment lest he should
fall overboard. Let them look at him ten times every night
to make sure he was safe from harm!

"Come northward to the court at once," the eager little
boy wrote "and bring with you this dwarf of the sacred
dances which you have brought alive and in good condition
from the Land of Ghosts, to please and delight the heart of
the King of Upper and Lower Egypt, who lives forever.

"When the dwarf goes with you on board the ship, appoint trustworthy people who shall remain very near him
on each side of the vessel and take care that he does not
fall into the water. When he sleeps at night, appoint trustworthy people who shall sleep beside him in his cabin and
look to see that he is safe ten times every night!

"My Majesty desires to see this dwarf more than all the
gifts from the mines of Sinai, or from the land of Punt!"

At length the pigmy arrived when the weather was at its

At the left Harkhuf with staff and wand of office and the dwarf, with a musical instrument. The royal cartouch means Pepi. To the right, a gate of the palace. In the lower right corner is Harkhuf. Opposite in the left corner is the dwarf, and in a room above sits the little King Pepi before a table. From Harkhuf's tomb at A-swan'.
From photographs taken by the Editor who crossed a strip of desert, climbed the steep cliff opposite Aswan, and visited the tomb. Very few travelers visit the lonely, deserted spot. Its interest is little known, and these pictures have never before been published.

hottest, and little boys, shut up indoors, longed most to be amused.

With all the impetuous ardor of a child who was later to be one of Egypt's most forceful kings, Pepi received the dwarf. The little black man did his dances like some little jointed doll, lending his tricks variety by screwing his face into grimaces as comical as those of the merry dwarf-god Bes.

And as to the great explorer, Harkhuf of Elephantine, he so prized his letter from the little child-Pharaoh Pepi, that he had it carved on the walls of his tomb, where it may be read to this day, the most human of all the documents that have come down from ancient Egypt, presenting a vivid picture of that eager little fellow who wore the crown of the Pharaohs four thousand five hundred years ago.

The Reign of Pepi II

Harkhuf's boy-Pharaoh, Pepi the Second, ruled longer than any king in history. For ninety years, at least, he sat on the throne of Egypt and during his reign the wild Negro tribes were ever more surely subdued, and Egypt's rule extended far up into Nubia.

The lifelike bronze head of Pepi I, father of Pepi II. Cairo Museum.

Moreover, the stout-hearted nobles of the Island of Elephantine were likewise sent to Punt, far to the south and eastward on the shores of the distant Red Sea, a very difficult journey whereon more than one bold adventurer sacrificed his life; for men had to cross the desert carrying lumber to build their boats, since there was no connection by water between the Red Sea and the Nile.

As the travellers constructed their vessels on the lonely shores of the sea, plunderers out of the desert often swept down upon them, forced them to fight for their lives, and more than once slew a few.

Adventuring abroad was the note of the times in Egypt. Some men went to the Land of Ghosts, some men went to Punt; some men went north to Sinai, and some launched their trading galleys to visit various islands that lay in the Great Green Sea, as they called the Mediterranean.

In time, Egyptian sailors landed on the island of Crete, a two or three day's sail north of the coast of Egypt.

They found Crete a picturesque place with customs all its own. There were ladies in ruffled skirts, that billowed out in the breeze. There were men with top-knots like coxcombs, and long locks hanging down on either side of their faces, men in gay-figured kilts with broad belts drawn in tight.

The Egyptians looked in on their sacred games, where boy

Egyptian sailors visit the island of Crete. They see women in full flounced skirts, men with curls and topknots, their waists drawn in tight by belts. They see pottery painted with fishes, and frescoes of toreadors, vaulting over bulls.

and girl toreadors caught huge bulls by their horns and went flying over their backs.

They saw priestesses of the serpent-goddess all twined about with snakes, and pottery in the markets painted with figures of fishes as became the dwellers on an isle.

But what most interested these Egyptian traders in Crete was the fact that the metal workers on this highly civilized island were far in advance of their own.

They forged their daggers of bronze, a metal new to the world, made of one part of tin to every nine parts of copper, and very much stronger than copper. Indeed the metal-workers of Crete proudly showed the Egyptians how one of their daggers of bronze could split a whole bar of copper.

From Crete Egyptian traders carried bronze back to Egypt, and henceforth for hundreds of years, weapons, tools, even furniture were made of this hard metal, bronze.

Mehenkwetre, one of the powerful nobles of the New or Middle Kingdom, an official of the Pharaoh Men'tu-ho'tep III, sits on his porch as slaves drive his cattle before him to count. A wooden model found in his tomb. This model and the figure of the dancing girl shown below are in the Metropolitan Museum, New York.

VIII

The Age of Too Powerful Nobles

(2475 B. C.—2000 B. C.)

Yearly the nobles of Egypt grew bolder, richer, more ambitious, through their daring adventures abroad until at last they threw off the rule of their Pharaohs, appearing as the first group of men in history to demand an extension of power beyond that of a king or a chief. But being jealous of each other, they created only confusion and strife.

The blue glazed earthenware figure of a tattooed dancing girl of dynasty XI, the age when the too powerful nobles were subdued. At the left the withered arm of a dancing girl's mummy showing the same tattooing.

135

All the glorious activities of the vigorous Old Kingdom vanished. No more did Egyptian vessels proudly ride the seas to bring home cedars from Lebanon or precious incense from Punt. No more did Egyptian miners heap up copper ore; for the mines in Sinai were silent. No more did Egyptian explorers push south up the Nile into Kush. The canals which Uni had built around the First Cataract fell to pieces and filled up with sand. The Black People crept further northward; Bed'ou-ins from the desert swarmed down into the Delta; in all Egypt's sorry domain were famine, disorder, robbery, violence, and distress.

Memphis, the Magnificent, the home of art and letters, sank into insignificance. Slowly the city of Thebes, heretofore considered only a backwoods village in a hinterland up the Nile, rose into leading place. A strong man named Men'tu-ho'tep came to the throne in Thebes, conquered the polished, elegant, superior folk of the North and made himself King of all Egypt. But the nobles remained all too powerful and it took a stronger man still, Pharaoh Am'en-em' het I, to deal with them and really give the land peace.

Mentuhotep of dynasty XI, who subdued the nobles; (from a stela.) Mentuhotep's wife with a maid handing her a jar of some sweet substance from which she fans away flies. (Queen's sarcophagus, Cairo Museum.)

Good times in the age of Amenemhet. Female acrobats and tumblers from tomb paintings at Be'ni Has'an. At the left, four groups are seen in difficult positions; next they take postures and finally leap into the air.

Amenemhet I, Founder of the Middle Kingdom

(TWELFTH DYNASTY, 2000–1970 B. C.)

Am'en-em'het I, founder of the famous twelfth dynasty, rose up as a savior. Though he could not entirely suppress the rebellious, aggressive nobles, he united them into a league owing allegiance to Pharaoh with the payment of taxes and service in war. He could not make them over into servants of the crown, as they had been in the days of the Pharaohs of the Old Kingdom, but he and his family were men so strong that they held this loose league together for some 200 years and prepared the way for Egypt to enter upon an age of even greater prosperity than that of the fine Old Kingdom. Amenemhet said of himself:

"I was one who cultivated grain and loved the harvest-god;
None was hungry in my years, none thirsted then;
Men dwelt in peace through that which I wrought."

Female jugglers toss balls in the air, play ball from the backs of companions, and throw a ball in time to the clapping of hands. Two men wrestlers take different holds. Twelfth dynasty paintings from Beni Hasan.

Little wooden models of a freight boat (right) and pleasure boat (left) found in the tomb of Mehenkwetre with other models showing all phases of a noble's life in the Middle Kingdom that he might have in his future life all he had been accustomed to on earth. (see page 135) When found, these models were covered with fly specks, mice marks and cobwebs which could not have come from the tomb where no fly or mouse could exist. It appears that they were kept by Mehenkwetre stored in an unused room of his house before being brought to his tomb, and since they are likewise covered with sticky finger marks, it is most probable that Mehenkwetre's children found the inviting toys, stole into the unused room and played with them. Metropolitan Museum, New York.

Before the royal asp on his brow, the rebellious were pacified; order returned to the land. He drove out the Asiatics who had swarmed down on the Delta to pasture their flocks and herds, and he built the great "Princes' Wall" to keep them out forever. Some say that Abraham, the Sem-it'ic chief of the Bible, was one of the Asiatics driven out by Amenemhet.

Wooden models of girls bringing baskets of wine and meats and carrying live ducks in their hands as offerings for the tomb of Mehenkwetre. Note that now in the New or Middle Kingdom, women are wearing gay figured garments in place of the plain, severe, simple white of the Old Kingdom. Note also the wide anklets and bracelets. Metropolitan Museum, New York.

But while from his palace of gold with ceilings of lapis-lazuli, Amenemhet kept watch over Egypt, a dark plot was hatched against him in his royal city Ith-to'we. The very people of his household, they who wore his linen and perfumed themselves with his myrrh, regarded him as their foe. After the evening meal, night having come, he once took an hour of heart's ease. Lying upon his couch, he relaxed his limbs, his mind began to follow slumber, when suddenly weapons were drawn and conspiracy was made against him. He awoke to fight alone. With his own hand, he seized the weapons of those who sought to slay him; he hurled them back; he saved his own life.

This miserable experience made the heart of the old king bitter. Henceforth he was sad and stern.

"Trust no man on earth," he said to his son, Se-sos'tris; and he raised Sesostris to the throne to share the burden of ruling. But while the Prince was away from home, fighting Libyans, news was brought him that Amenemhet had died, "gone down to the Hills of the West," as Egyptians said.

Immediately, plots arose to make another royal son, instead of Sesostris, King; but Sesostris left his army and hurried home so swiftly that he got himself crowned in safety.

To this day, there remains a true story telling about this event, and how a certain Sin'-u-he ran away from Egypt for fear lest he be suspected of having a part in the plot.

Sinuhe fled to Canaan, in days very near the time of Abraham, chief of the Hebrews. The chiefs whom he met in Ca'naan lived exactly as Abraham did, and looked like "Absha, a ruler of the Hill Country," whom a powerful Egyptian noble had painted on his tomb at Beni Hasan.

Absha, a prince of Canaan, who came down into Egypt with 37 followers, bearing cosmetics and eye-salve. From a twelfth dynasty tomb at Beni Hasan. For the train of his followers, see V. II, 98. Such a prince was Abraham.

A pectoral or breast ornament of Sesostris II, beautifully enamelled in colors, showing the hawk-headed lions beneath the protecting vulture of Egypt destroying the Libyans of the western desert. Cairo Museum. (See page 127.)

The Adventures of Sinuhe*

In the thirtieth year of his reign, King Amenemhet I went down to the Hills of the West. The palace was hushed and men's hearts were filled with sorrow. The great gates were closed; the courtiers sat with bowed heads; the people wept for his death.

Now his Majesty had dispatched an army into the western desert against the Libyan tribesmen, his eldest son being commander of it, the good god-Prince Sesostris; but just as Sesostris was returning, having taken captives from the Libyans and cattle without limit, the Peers of the Court sent messengers to inform him of the sad event that had taken place at the palace, and these messengers met him on his way home, reaching him at the time of evening.

*Given in a *History of the Pharaohs* by Arthur Weigall and in *Egyptian Tales, First Series*, by W. M. Flinders Petrie. Also described in *A History of Egypt*, by J. H. Breasted who says: "The unfortunate noble, Sinuhe, who fled into Syria on the death of Amenemhet I, returned to Egypt in his old age, and the story of his flight, of his life and adventures in Asia, became a favorite tale, which attained such popularity that it was even written on sherds and flags of stone to be placed in the tomb for the entertainment of the dead in the hereafter."

Without a moment's delay, the new King, Sesostris, the Hawk, flew away with a few attendants. This he did in secret that he might return to Egypt and be hailed at once as King. And he said: "Tell not this news to my troops," for he feared lest one of the Princes who was with him in his army, might set himself up as King.

Nevertheless, a message had been privately sent to the Princes, and one of these had already been hailed by his soldiers as Pharaoh. Now I, Sinuhe, the friend of Amenemhet and a greatly favored attendant upon his wife, the Queen, stood in the darkness when I overheard this prince plotting.

Sesostris I, the Prince of this story. From a wall carving at Captos. Now at University College, London. Sesostris is the Greek form of this King's name. In Egyptian it is written Senusert or Sesusri.

Then my heart stopped beating and trembling seized all my limbs lest I should be suspected of having plotted.

I rushed for a hiding place, and betook myself to the bushes on either side of the road, to separate my path from that of any traveller. I crossed the Fa-yum' lake and came to the island of Snefru, where I lay in the fields all night.

When day came, I went on again, till a man rose up from my path; but he was afraid and dismayed when he saw that I was one obliged to flee from Egypt. So I reached the town of Negeu near the hour of the evening meal; I crossed the Nile in a rudderless boat, a west wind helping me, and I made my way into the desert past the shrine of the hill-goddess, Lady of the Red Mountain.

Wooden models of Egyptian soldiers of the Twelfth Dynasty just such as those led by Prince Sesostris into Lib'y-a. From the tomb of a Prince of As-yut', now in the Cairo Museum. The Egyptians are spearmen, with bronze tipped spears. The shields are each painted in a different way so that each man may recognize his own equipment.

Thereafter, I went northwards, letting my feet follow their own path, and when several days had passed, I arrived at the Wall of the Prince, which had been made by the late King to hold back the Bedouins and to check the desert-wanderers. I crawled into the bushes, for fear lest I should be seen by the sentinels of the day-watch who patrolled the top of the fortress. At nightfall, I crossed the wall, and I arrived at Pe-ten' as dawn was brightening the land.

Thirst hasted me on and on. I dried up; my throat narrowed. I fell exhausted and said: "This is the taste of death!"

Black E'thi-o'pi-an bowmen from the same tomb as the above. The loin cloth of the Ethiopian is much shorter than the white kilt of the Egyptian and is colored in different ways. These soldiers carry bows and arrows.

But when I had lifted up my heart and gathered strength, I heard a voice and the lowing of cattle, and presently I beheld some Bedouins approaching. Now there was a chieftain amongst them who had been in Egypt, and he recognized me. He gave me water, he boiled me some milk, and I went with him to his tribe. These people treated me well; one tribe sent me on to another, till I came to the land of E'dom, where I dwelt for half a year. Then the Prince of the Tribes sent for me, and I was taken before Enshi-Amusi, Prince of Upper Syria, and the Great Prince said:

"If you will remain with me, you can hear your own language of Egypt. But tell me, why have you come hither? Has aught occurred at the Palace of the Pharaoh?"

I replied: "Amenemhet has gone down to the Hills of the West, and none knows what is come to pass as a result of his going." And I also said: "I was coming back from the war with the Libyans, when a certain piece of news became known to me, at which my brain reeled, and my mind was no longer in my body, but led me away on the desert road. Yet nobody had spoken ill of me, nobody spat in my face. I really do not know what brought me to this land."

Then the Prince said: "What will Egypt do without King Amenemhet, who made all nations respect him?"

I said to him in answer: "His son, Sesostris, has entered the Palace, and has taken up the inheritance of his father, and Sesostris is a master of wisdom, prudent in his designs, with good-will to him who goes or to him who comes."

To this the Prince replied: "Egypt is happy then. But you?—You are far from Egypt. You shall stay here with me and I will entreat you well."

Then he married me to his eldest daughter and let me choose as a home the best part of his land; and I chose the land of Ya, a goodly, pleasant place, wherein figs and grapes abounded. Copious was its honey, many were its olives, and all kinds of fruit were on its trees. Wheat and barley grew there, and there were flocks and herds innumerable.

Great also was that which afterwards fell to my portion by reason of the affection lavished on me by the Prince of Syria. He made me chieftain of a tribe of the best people of his country. Food was provided by them for my daily fare, and wine for my daily needs; cooked flesh and roast fowl, too, were provided; for men hunted animals in the neighboring desert, and laid them before me, in addition to those which were caught by my dogs. And milk-foods were sent to me, prepared in all sorts of ways.

I dwelled in a tent surrounded by the tents of my people. I let my hair and beard grow after the manner of the people of Syria. I slept on the ground, and not on a bed.

Many years I spent thus. Any Egyptian envoy who was

travelling north, or returning south to the Palace of the Pharaoh, stayed with me, for I made all men stay as my guests. I gave water to the thirsty; him who had lost his way I set upon the road; and I rescued him who had been robbed. My sons grew up into fine men, and each became chief of a tribe.

When the Bedouins became insolent and opposed the rulers of the desert, I led the men of my Prince; I made war on all sides. Every tribe against which I marched was driven from its pasturage and its wells. I seized its cattle, I took captive its people, doing this by my own strong arm, and by my clever strategy.

I became a favorite in the Prince's heart, and he loved me, and noted my pluck, and set me in command of his people, higher even than the place of his own children.

Once there came a mighty man of Syria and defied me in my tent. He was a champion of the Tenu bold without equal, one who had terrorized the whole of Syria; and he had sworn that he would fight me; for he planned to steal my cattle for his tribe.

The Prince took counsel with me, and I said: "I do not know this fellow. Have I ever walked about his camping-place? Have I ever opened his gate or knocked down a fence of his? No, he defies me for envy because I carry out your wishes. However, if his heart is set on a fight, then let him stand forth and challenge me."

That night I strung my bow and tested my arrows, drew my dagger, and sharpened my weapons. At dawn the land of the Tenu came together. It had gathered its tribes and called all the neighboring people. It spoke of nothing but the fight. Out came the champion towards me and I took up my stand facing him. Every heart ached for me, the women and men all talking at once; for they said: "Is there any man strong enough to fight this man of Tenu? Behold,

he hath a shield, a battle-axe, and an armful of javelins!"

But I drew him to the attack. He launched his armful of javelins and I dodged them all in safety. I turned aside his arrows and they struck the ground in vain. Then we drew near, the one to the other. He fell upon me and I shot him. I shot an arrow into his neck, and he uttered a yell and fell on his nose. I killed him with his own battle-axe, and, standing on his back, uttered a shout of triumph.

Then the Asiatics shrieked; but I and the people whom he had oppressed gave thanks to Mentu, the war-god, and Prince Enshi-Amusi embraced me. I carried off the dead man's possessions, and rounded up his cattle. I seized what was in his tent, and ransacked his camp.

Owing to this, I became an important man, and I grew great in wealth, and rich in flocks. I was a man who left his country because of nakedness; but now I was clad in white clothes and fine linen. Many were my servants; beautiful was my dwelling place, wide were my estates; and above all, the memory of me was in the Palace in Egypt.

Nevertheless, I prayed: "O God, whichever god thou art,

who hast ordained this flight of mine, show mercy, and bring
me back to the Palace, unto the place where my heart dwells;
for what thing is more important than that my body should
be buried in the land where I was born? Though an happy
lot hath befallen me, yet old age approaches, my hands are
weak, my heart is weary. O, let the King of Egypt show
mercy to me, that I may greet once more the Lady of the
Land, the Queen-mother in his Palace! O, let me serve my
sovereign Lady once again, and let her talk to me about her
children's beauty!"

Then Sesostris, the King of Egypt, was told of my situation, and his Majesty sent me gifts with greetings from the
Royal Children, as though I had been the Prince of some
foreign land: "This lady, the Queen-mother, who is heaven
itself to you, is still living and in good health," he wrote.
"She has her part in the sovereignty of the land, and her
children are at court. May you long enjoy the good things
that she shall give you, and may you live by her bounty!

"Come to Egypt, that you may see the Palace wherein
you grew up, and that you may do homage at the great
doorways, and take your place amongst my Peers. Think
of the day of burial when you pass to the Realms of the
Blessed! Think what a funeral procession we will arrange for
you! Your mummy-case shall be of gold, with head of lapis-
lazuli! You shall be placed upon the hearse, oxen drawing

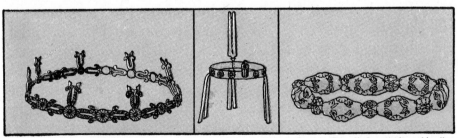

The Queen and princesses Sinuhe so longed to see, may have had jewels like this. Two diadems and a gold collar
of lion heads belonging to princesses of the 12th Dynasty, the age of Sesostris and Sinuhe. Cairo Museum.

A funeral procession such as Sinuhe longed for. From the tomb of a nobleman of his period, at Beni Hasan. The statue of the nobleman in its "naos" is dragged by 7 men. Three men beat time for the dancers shown on the next page

you along; and the sacred dance of the Muu shall be performed at the mouth of your tomb. You shall not die abroad; Asiatic tribesmen shall not be your escort. You shall not be wrapped in a sheepskin and buried in the sand!"

This letter reached me as I stood amongst my tribesmen. It was read aloud to me, and I flung myself down on my face and threw dust on my hair. Then I went about my encampment rejoicing and crying: "Sweet, indeed, is thy graciousness, O King, which grants that the last rites for my body shall be carried out at home!"

Then I answered the royal letter and said: "As regards the flight which I made in my stupidity, I did not plan it; it was not in my mind; I do not know what separated me from my home. It happened like a dream, as when a man of Lower Egypt sees himself at El-e-phan-tine'."

Soon there came unto me envoys of the god-King Sesostris. I made a feast for my children. My eldest son became the leader of my tribe. All my goods passed to him and I gave him my cattle, my fruit, and all my pleasant trees.

Then I set out southwards, and journeyed to the frontier of Egypt, where the commanding officer in charge of the frontier-patrol sent a message off to the Palace. His Majesty sent his trusted Chief Huntsman to me, having with him boats filled with presents of the royal bounty for the

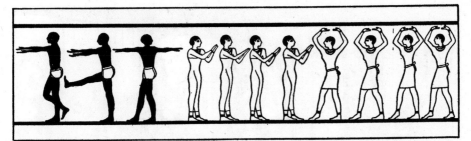

The three last men on the preceding page are beating time for the male dancers shown here. Behind the men-dancers are women beating time for women-dancers. Behind these were shown men bringing clothing, ornaments, etc.

Asiatics of my escort. The brewers of the town squeezed and strained the beer in my presence; we held a farewell feast for my friends of the Syrian tribes. I parted from the Syrians, and sailed up the river to Ith-to'we; and at dawn ten men came to meet me and convey me to the palace.

Soon I was bending my head to the ground between the sphinxes, while the Royal Princes stood at the gateway awaiting my coming. The Peers in the courtyard pointed out the way to the Audience-hall; and I found his Majesty on his great throne in the hall of pale gold. I flung myself on my face and my wits forsook me, although the King greeted me graciously. My soul fled, my flesh trembled!

Therefore his Majesty said to one of his nobles: "Lift him up, and let him speak to me!" And his Majesty said: "So you have come,—you who have trodden the deserts and wandered in the wilderness!"

Nevertheless, I was afraid. The dread in my heart was like that which had caused my fateful flight.

Then the royal family were summoned and likewise the Queen-mother. And his Majesty said: "This is Sinuhe, who is come home as an Asiatic, a son of the Bedouin!"

Thereat the Queen uttered a cry, and the Royal Children shouted out all together, saying: "It cannot really be he!"

But his Majesty said: "It is really he!"

The family then begged Pharaoh to show me favor. The Royal Children shook their sistra and sang:

"May thy hands prosper, O King;
  Grant good things to this traveller, Sinuhe, born in the land of Egypt,—
Who fled away from fear of thee,
Who fled this land from thy terrors!"

And Pharaoh said: "Let him not fear, for he shall be one of my Peers. Take him now to the dressing-room!"

Thus, when I had left the Audience-hall, the Royal Children gave me their hands, and we went together through the great doorway, and I was taken into the house of one of the Royal Princes. There was splendid furniture in it, and a bathroom with painted scenes on its walls. Robes of royal material were in every room, perfumes, and precious ointment; and every servant busied himself with his task.

The years were made to pass away from my flesh; my beard was shaved, and my hair was combed. My bundle was thrown out into the desert; my clothes were given to the sand-dwellers; and I was clad in soft linen and anointed with precious ointment. At night I lay upon a bed once more, and I gave up the sand to those that live in it.

There was given to me the house of a lord of slaves, which had belonged to a royal friend. My meals were brought to me from the Palace three and four times a day, besides that which the Royal Children were constantly giving me. And a tomb of stone was constructed for me in the midst of the pyramids. There were given to me peasants; there were made for me a garden and fields in it before my house. My funeral statue was inlaid with gold, its girdle of pale gold; Pharaoh caused it to be made.

May I be in the favor of Pharaoh, son of the Sun-god, the great god-King, until the day shall come of my death!

Sinuhe looks at himself to see the change in his appearance while an attendant carries off his Asiatic woolen garments. The mirror is a real silver mirror of the period with handle of black obsidian and gold Hathor head.

The Powerful Twelfth Dynasty

(2000–1788 B. C.)

A portrait statue of Sesostris III, the great warrior king of Greek legends. (Now in the British Museum.)

Sesostris I, the King of Sinuhe's story, carried on with undimmed splendor the glory of his line. Under Amenemhet II and Sesostris II, the black men were driven back, the mines in Sinai were opened, and traffic was once more resumed with the far off land of Punt; moreover the Pharaohs dug a canal to connect the Red Sea with the Nile, so that traders no more used the dangerous desert-route, but now went by ship to Punt.

Sesostris III, like Sesostris I, was a mighty warrior-king, who led all his wars in person.

Through the hard barrier of rocks that formed the First Cataract, Sesostris cut a canal, to replace the canals of Uni which had by now disappeared. Thus he could take his war-galleys up against the Black People; and he conquered all the land even as far southward as the Second Cataract, where he built two mighty fortresses and set up boundary stones forbidding Negroes to pass that point.

Sesostris III now ruled 1000 miles of Nile Valley. Furthermore, he was the first King of Egypt to make an invasion of Asia, raiding the land of Canaan. Indeed, Sesostris III was so great a king that, after his death, his figure loomed larger and larger in the wonder-tales of his people, until in Greek legends he appears no more than a hero of myths.

Statues of Amenemhet III, the first as a sweet-faced young man (Cairo Museum), the second as he grows older and sterner (Berlin), the last as an old man weighed down with cares and sorrows (Macgregor collection).

The son of Sesostris III was Am-en-em'het III, a king who devoted himself to increasing Egypt's resources, rather than to warring at home or in foreign lands.

In Sinai, Amenemhet built barracks for the miners with houses for officials, and strong, stone fortifications to protect the mines from the Bedouins, that Egyptian workmen might now live permanently at the mines, instead of being sent out on camping expeditions. Thus Amenemhet made copper mining a fixed and stable industry.

And Amenemhet helped the farmers no less than he did the miners. For there existed near the Nile a valley called the Fa-yum', into which the river flowed whenever its waters were high, making a lake called Lake Moeris. Amenemhet built a great wall twenty-seven miles long, which dammed this water up, keeping it in smaller space, reclaiming thousands of acres

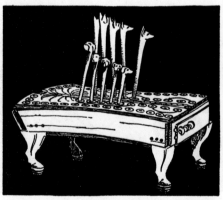

An ivory game-board of Amenemhet's time, 12th Dynasty, with animal-headed pegs, used like a cribbage board. Interesting evidence of the antiquity of such games. Carnarvon Collection.

of land which could now be planted with grain, and holding
the water stored against the drought of the summer time,
when gates in the wall were opened, and the water was
allowed to pass out and run off to the farms.

So deeply interested was Amenemhet in this work in
the Fayum that Croc'o-dil-op'o-lis, the city which grew up
on the land reclaimed from the river, became his favorite
residence. There he built an enormous building, 800 feet
wide and 1000 feet long, a vast labyrinth of rooms, which
became the center of government,—for in it each district of
Egypt had its separate hall, where its particular gods were
enshrined and where, from time to time, its rulers held their
councils. Concerning Amenemhet the people of Egypt sang:

"He maketh the Two Lands verdant more than a great Nile,
    He hath filled the Two Lands with strength.
    The treasures he gives are food for those who follow him!"

The beginning of the drama in Egypt in the Middle kingdom. Priests at A-by'dos present to eager spectators a play
showing the life of Osiris. After all his adventures, Osiris sits at last supreme. Beside him are his wife Isis and his
son Horus, the hawk-headed god, while a priest makes an offering before them. The spectators are as anxious to
see as the audience at a modern play.

Thus the Twelfth Dynasty and the Middle Kingdom brought growth and good times to Egypt. Books and writing flourished. There were books of stories, books of travel, poems, fables, essays, and even the very first plays ever known in the world. For at A-by'dos, priests acted out with elaborate show in the temples the Life and Death of Osiris, thereby originating the first dramas ever presented.

The life of the court and nobles found reflection among the people, in folk tales adorning with marvelous fancies the plain facts of their history. One of these ancient tales, full of the thrill of sea-voyages and the mystery of Punt, is

The Story of the Shipwrecked Sailor*

I was going down to the mines on a mission of the King, and I rode the Great Green Sea in a ship 150 cubits in length and 40 cubits in breadth, and in it were 150 sailors, picked men of Egypt. They scanned the heavens and they

*The original papyrus of this ancient combination of Robinson Crusoe and Sinbad the Sailor is now in the National Museum at Leningrad. It is the oldest known story book in the world. A cubit is 1½ feet.

scanned the earth and their hearts were stouter than lions. There was none unproven amongst them. The storm arose while we were in the Great Green Sea, and as we sailed, it redoubled its strength. The waves thereof were eight cubits.

The ship perished and of them that were in her, not one was left save me.

I clung to a plank of wood. The wood was cast on a Phantom Isle that floated on the waters. Beneath it moved the seas; the underhalf was waves. I passed three days alone with only my heart as companion, sleeping in the midst of a thicket. Then the storm subsided and the sun shone once again.

Straightway I employed my legs in search of something for my mouth. I found figs and grapes with vegetables; I found berries, nuts and melons, I found fish and birds,—naught was lacking. I satisfied my hunger and threw away what was left. I dug a ditch, I lit a fire, I sacrificed to the gods.

Then I heard a voice like thunder. The trees trembled, the earth shook; and lo, a serpent approached me. This serpent was thirty cubits long; his beard hung down for two cubits; his body was as if encrusted with gold on the blue of lapis lazuli. He planted himself before me, and thus he spake while I stayed dumbfounded:

"What hath brought thee, what hath brought thee, little one? What hath brought thee to this isle that is in the midst of the sea? If thou delayest to tell me, thou shalt disappear like a flame!"

He seized me in his mouth; he carried me to his lair; he laid me down unharmed; and I said:

"I was going down to the mines on a mission of the King, and a storm arose on the Sea. The ship perished, and of them that were in her, not one was left save me. I clung to a plank of wood, which was cast on this isle by the waves."

Thereupon the Serpent said to me: "Fear not, fear not, little one, let not thy face show sorrow. Behold! thou shalt pass month after month with me until thou hast stayed four months; then a ship shall come with sailors and thou shalt return and embrace thy wife and little ones again. Meantime talk and be happy. I am here surrounded by my brothers and children, 75 serpents in all. We had, too, a little girl whom Fortune sent me, but on her, alack, the fire of heaven fell and she was burned to ashes."

Then I touched the ground before him and said: "I shall describe thee to Pharaoh and make thy greatness known to him. For thee I shall slay asses in sacrifice. I shall send ships to thee filled with all the marvels of Egypt."

But he smiled and answered: "I am lord of Punt and need naught of what thou offerest me. Moreover, when once thou leavest this isle, never shalt thou see it again, for it shall be changed into waves."

And I dwelt four months on the Isle of the Double, where naught was lacking. It was filled with all good things. Then, behold, a ship appeared as the Serpent had predicted. I perched myself in a tree to try to see who were on it. I hastened to tell the Serpent the news, but I found that he knew it already; and he said to me: "Good journey, good journey home, little one."

Then I bent before him with low-hanging arms, and he gave me presents of essences, offertory perfume, pomade, cinnamon, thuya, sapan wood, powdered antimony, cypress, ordinary incense in great quantities, elephants' teeth, greyhounds, baboons, green monkeys, and all kinds of good and precious things. I put all on board the ship that had come, and prostrating myself, I offered him worship.

He said: "Behold, in two months thou shalt be home!"

And after that, I went down towards the ship and called

to the sailors on board. I gave thanks on the shore to the
lord of the isle and likewise to the five and seventy serpents.

And we sailed away from the isle and came in the second
month, just as the Serpent had said, unto the City of Pharaoh. I entered into the palace and gave Pharaoh all the
presents I had brought away from that island, and he
uttered his thanks to me before all the assembled people.
Then he set me on high amongst his Peers.

This is taken from beginning to end as it is found in the
book. Who has written it is the scribe with nimble fingers,—
Ameni-Amen-aa,—Life, Health, Strength!

The Shepherd Kings Conquer Egypt

(ABOUT 1675 B. C.)

After Amenemhet III had passed to the Realms of the Sun God the nation quickly declined. Pretender after pretender struggled for the throne, until once again Egypt broke up into many petty kingdoms.

Then a dark storm cloud rose in the North, threatening death and destruction. Down on this land in confusion came a hungry horde of barbarians led by the Hyk'sos or Shepherd Kings. Savage, swarthy, hard-featured, black-bearded warriors, they came from Mes'o-po-ta'mi-a, Syria, Scythia and Arabia, and they had often before come down to pasture their herds in the Delta. It was to keep them out that Amenemhet I had built the Prince's Wall.

Against these wild barbarians, Egypt, so disunited, could make no effective resistance. District after district passed under their fierce sway, never daring to give them battle. They robbed and burned and plundered. They took men, women and children captive and carried them off as slaves. "Scourges of Mankind, Filthy Ones," the Egyptians called them; but the "Filthy Ones" conquered

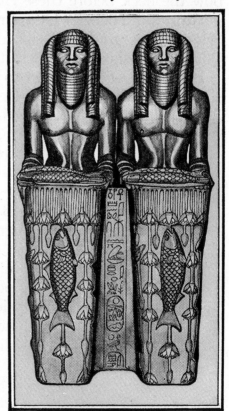

The Hyksos must have looked like this. Restored from two barbaric statues in the Cairo Museum. These statues are utterly unlike Egyptians in features, wig and typical Asiatic beard. See also Vol. II, p. 115.

the Delta, established themselves at A-var′is, and proclaimed the most important of their barbarous chieftains as King. The sleek, clean-shaven Egyptians had to accept the rule of these shaggy, black-bearded herdsmen and acknowledge their chieftain as Pharaoh. For a hundred years or more they ruled the land of Egypt, gradually growing civilized and learning the customs of Egypt.

Of the few scattered petty kingdoms that even after a hundred years still maintained independence and refused to bow the neck before these Herdsmen Kings, the most important was Thebes. Up the river at Thebes the young king, Sek-en-en′re, and his vigorous little mother, the proud Queen Tet-i-sher′i, still held their heads very high.

It was a poor little court to which Tetisheri had come as a slim and lovely young bride. Thebes was a beggared city,

the last hope of the Egyptians, whither refugees flocked from all the Egyptian towns that had been seized and sacked by the onslaughts of the foe. But even as a widow and a grandmother, the Queen was the very spirit of high-handed independence, and proud opposition to the foe. She married her son Sekenenre to one of her daughters, Ah-ho′tep, and directed the course of affairs.

And A-po′pi, the King of the Herdsmen, seeing the determined spirit that still continued to live in the little Southern Kingdom, decided by some

A charming statue of Queen Tetisheri, the moving spirit of resistance to the Herdsmen. This statue is now in the British Museum, London.

means or other to force a quarrel with the King; so he called his chiefs to deliberate concerning what message to send him.

Now Apopi had made the evil god Set his chief god and served no other god of the whole land but Set. And the hippopotami which the princes of Thebes delighted to hunt were sacred to this god Set; so the wisemen advised Apopi that he should send to Sekenenre bidding him refrain from committing the terrible sacrilege of hunting the hippopotami, saying that those outraged creatures destroyed his sleep at night by reason of their complaining!

Messengers therefore took this outrageous command to the King, and by that means or some other, they succeeded at last in bringing about an open war with Thebes.

Urged on by his vigorous mother, the valiant King Sekenenre plunged into war with the Herdsmen. He had to arouse his people, by nature so unwarlike, to determined, persistent effort. He had to fight with a foe who brought horses and chariots for the first time into Egypt and rode their enemies down beneath their snorting steeds.

But in the midst of this struggle, a grim and terrible tragedy put an end to the young King's life. He may have been at the front at war with the barbarians, or he may have been in his palace, a victim of palace intrigues; but as his mummy shows by its yawning wounds and agonized limbs, his enemies caught him unawares, either creep-

The mummy of King Sekenenre, showing a wound in the skull, other yawning wounds, the teeth gritted and lips drawn up in agony, telling the whole tale of his death and hasty burial. This tragic mummy is now preserved in the Cairo Museum.

Queen Tetisheri urges her son, Sekenenre to rebel as the Hyksos messenger presents his preposterous command that they still the roaring of the hippopotami so that it may not disturb the sleep of the Hyksos king.

ing up behind him and striking him down so swiftly that he did not even have time to lift a hand in his own defense, or falling upon him in his sleep, battering him with a battle axe, hacking him with sword and spear, then rudely bundling his mangled corpse in the wrappings of its grave clothes and rushing it off to the tomb, not even taking the trouble to straighten his clawing hands and his painful distorted lips.

Tetisheri's son was dead and the final storm of the Hyksos invasion was just about to break, but the influence of the Queen was still alive in the palace.

Kem'ose, the newly hailed Pharaoh, was either the Queen's son or grandson, and under the urge of her spirit, he made up his mind to attack the invading Herdsmen anew. So he called his Council of Peers and said: "To what purpose am I King when there is one chieftain in Avaris and another in Kush? I sit here with an Asiatic on one side and a Negro on the other, while every man holds his own slice of this Egypt. I shall grapple with these Asiatics! I shall rip open their bellies!"

But the Peers said: "It is true that the Asiatics put out their tongues at us altogether; however, we are at ease here holding our part of Egypt. Wait until they attack us. Then will be time enough for us to rise up and fight them."

Words of such cowardly weakness roused Kemose to a fury.

"As to this advice of yours," he cried, trembling with indignation; "I will fight the Asiatics!"

And he gathered together a band of the fierce, black fighting Ma'zois and sailed in his boats down stream.

"Every warrior was before me like a flame of fire," he cried, "and the troops of the Mazoi advanced to search out the Asiatics. East and West, we were victorious! I spent the night on my ship, and when the day dawned, I pounced like

King Kemose, with Egyptian and Ethiopian warriors, defeats the Hyksos in their chariots. The Hyksos first introduced the use of the horse to Egypt. Being mixed Asiatic tribes, they brought the horse from Asia where it had been in use for about 400 years. The Kassites were the horse-breeders who sold horses to all of Asia. See Vol. II, p. 24.

a hawk on the enemy, a cowardly Egyptian princeling who made common cause with the Herdsmen. I found him perfuming his mouth. I knocked down his walls! I slaughtered his people!"

Thus Kemose won back from the invaders the main part of Upper Egypt, and prospects were bright for regaining the whole of the conquered land. But at that moment Kemose died, and Ah'mose, the youngest son of the late King Sekenenre, and grandson of Queen Tetisheri, came to the throne of Egypt, a youth of about sixteen.

The father, the brother, the uncles of Ahmose,—all were dead. There were no royal men at the court of Thebes to surround the youthful Pharaoh, but there were three determined women, Nof-re-ti'ri, his wife and sister, Ahhotep, his mother, and his grandmother, Tetisheri. Under their vigorous influence, Ahmose continued with courage the war against the Hyksos, leading his own hosts to battle, driving the Herdsmen before him, and shutting them up at last within their strong fortress, Avaris, which lifted its threatening walls above the green fields of the Delta.

For three years Ahmose continued in camp, laying siege to Avaris, and twice in that time the Herdsmen sent war-galleys out of the city by way of a narrow canal in a desperate effort to get much needed supplies to Avaris. But the watchful fleet of Ahmose gave the enemy battle and destroyed them or drove them back.

"Now the King was besieging the city of Avaris," says Ahmose-son-of-Ebana, a naval commander in Pharaoh's fleet, "and I fought on foot before his Majesty, in consequence of which I was appointed to the battleship, *Crowned-in-Memphis*. Then the King fought on the waters of the canal, called the Waterway of Avaris, and I fought in single combat and killed the enemy and cut off his hand. It was reported to the King's recorder, and the King presented me with gold for my valor. Then again on a second occasion, there was fighting on the canal."

And so after three long years, Avaris was forced to surrender. The Herdsmen poured out of their city and fled up northward toward Canaan, pursued by the hosts of Pharaoh, who scattered them to the four winds.

Then Ahmose, the King, the liberator of Egypt from the power of the Herdsmen invaders, returned in triumph to Thebes, defeated his other enemies in Nubia and Egypt, and restored the land to peace and prosperity again.

Thus the old Queen Tetisheri lived to see Thebes transformed from a little provincial city into the flourishing capital of a great and powerful Empire, and she received a gift of lands retaken from the Herdsmen. There, on her own estates, she lived in comfort and peace for all the rest of her days, and when at last she died, an overseer placed in her chapel a pair of beautiful statues, picturing her as the charming, slim, little Princess she was when she came as a bride to Thebes.

The great King Ahmose himself never forgot his vigorous, proud and handsome little grandmother, who had directed three generations of his family through the course of the Hyksos wars; and even toward the end of his reign, he recorded on a stone tablet his deep devotion to her.

At last the Princes of Thebes had driven out the Herdsmen and paved the way for the rise of the powerful Empire of Egypt.

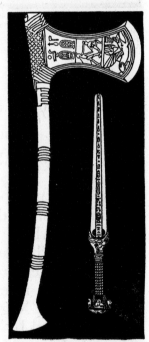

Bronze battle axe and dagger of Ahmose I, the conqueror of the Hyksos. They are inlaid with designs in gold and set with costly stones. A portrait of the king seizing an enemy by the hair may be seen on his battle axe. Cairo Museum.

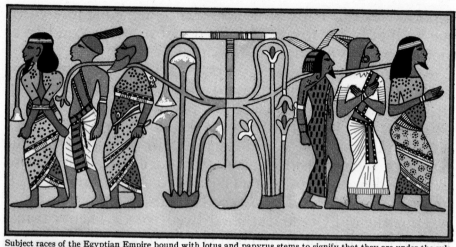

Subject races of the Egyptian Empire bound with lotus and papyrus stems to signify that they are under the rule of Egypt. First to the left is an Asiatic (a Canaanite or an Amorite), next is a Negro; third, another Asiatic, red-headed and red-bearded, probably a Syrian. Fourth in the long red robe is a tattooed Libyan from the Western desert, with his hair cut in a peculiar way and two feathers in his hair; fifth is another Negro and last another Asiatic. The papyrus and lotus plants signify the union of the Two Lands of Egypt (from El Amarna).

IX

Egypt, the First Great Empire

THUTMOSE I (1557–1501 B. C.)

The family of Ahmose, the brilliant eighteenth dynasty, transformed Egypt from a little kingdom into a mighty Empire with numberless subject states. The granddaughter of Ahmose married the warlike Thut'mose, a short, stocky, little man, whose title was Mighty Bull and Strong-like-Amon. On the death of Am-en-ho'tep I, this Thutmose fell heir to the throne, and he set out at once up the Nile to extend the rule of Egypt beyond the Third Cataract.

"I held the Negroes of Nubia helpless in my grip," he cried, "dazzled by my fame, powerless before the gleaming cobra that flamed on my royal forehead. Among them I was like a young panther amongst a herd in flight. There remained not a man of all the 'People-of-the-crimpy-hair' who dared to come against me!"

Then he sailed downstream again, with the body of a miserable Nubian chief, slain by him in combat, hanging upside down at the prow of his royal ship.

And having subdued the Southland, he turned northward to Canaan and Syria. He conquered the stiff-necked princes. He crossed the Lebanon mountains and set up his boundary stone on the banks of the river Euphrates, where men had never looked on Egyptian soldiers before.

His empire reached from the lands of the wild, naked Negro

Amenhotep I, son of Ahmose, the Great, and father of the Queen who married Thutmose I, grasping an Asiatic and a Negro captive by the hair and wielding a battle axe, thus showing the beginnings of Empire. A pectoral or breast ornament found on the body of a baby boy about a year old, the son of Amenhotep.

chieftains, sweltering in the sun beyond the Third Cataract, to the far-away Euphrates, land of woolen garments, beyond which Assyria lay.

Through the dark days of struggle against the invading Herdsmen, the people of Egypt, before so mild, had turned themselves into warriors, and under this born fighter, Thutmose, they were ready to sally forth and conquer the whole of the world.

The young men all were warriors,—let foreign slaves do the building,—Egyptians yearned for adventure. Already they had felt the thrill of seeing strange new lands,—rude mud huts in Nubia; little walled towns in Canaan, perched up high on the hills; black goats'-hair tents of Bed'ou-ins, squatting on the sands. They had chased most curious people,—pale-faced, tattooed Libyans, Negroes with feather head-dresses, black-bearded Asiatics wrapped in long, fringed garments, the women carrying their babies in baskets on their backs. And nowhere had they found a tribe that could stand before the ranks of Pharaoh's well-drilled army, with its chariots and horses, its strong and powerful regiments of shining Negro warriors.

Egypt at last had become a military nation. The youth of Egypt was all aflame with the glamorous love of war.

The First Great Woman of History

HATSHEPSUT (Hot-shep'soot) 1501–1480 B. C.

Now, though Thutmose I had many children born of less royal wives, he had only one child by Ahmose, his Great Royal Wife and Queen. This daughter, named Hatshepsut, was the old man's darling and pet.

The girl was a vivid creature, strong and energetic, full of her father's spirit and a worthy great, great granddaughter of the able Queen Tetisheri. Among all the sons of Thutmose, there was none of such force and fire. As to Thutmose II, elegant, weak and refined, the care of his toe-nails and finger-nails was more to him than the Empire. And yet it was this young dandy whom the people would be most apt to hail as the King of Egypt when Thutmose the elder was dead.

As the sturdy old warrior advanced in years, he wished to make sure that Hatshepsut should follow him on the throne. The power of women in Egypt had always been very great. Through women estates were handed down and rarely did a king of the land feel his claim to the throne complete until he had married his sister or other female heir. But to have a woman as Pharaoh was quite a different matter. No woman had ruled the land since the days of Queen Nitokris, a thousand years before. And so when the little Princess reached the age of fifteen, her father determined to name her before all the court as his heir. Calling her to him, he said:

"Come, glorious one! I have brought you before me that you may assume your royal dignity. Your forehead shall be adorned with the diadem of Upper and Lower Egypt."

Then he caused to be summoned the Captains of the King, the nobles, peers and officers of the court, with the chief of the people, to pay homage unto her. And he held a sitting in his audience-hall while the people prostrated themselves before him. And he said:

"This is my daughter Hatshepsut; I have appointed her to be my successor upon my glorious throne."

And the people, hearing this royal word, kissed the earth at Pharaoh's feet and thanked all the gods. And they went forth with mouths rejoicing and published his proclamation. All the people of all the departments of the Court heard it and came, their mouths rejoicing. Soldier cried it to soldier. They jumped and danced for the double joy of their hearts. They proclaimed the name of her Majesty as their future sovereign even while her Majesty was still no more than a child. And all the people were united upon the selection of her as their sovereign.

Nevertheless, when Thutmose died only a short time later, Hatshepsut found these same people stubbornly determined to have no young girl rule them, altogether unwilling to make her their queen in fact.

Then began the long struggle of the first great woman in history to overcome the prejudice in the minds of the mass of men. She was obliged at once to marry her brother Thutmose to make good her right to the crown.

But when Hatshepsut had set the elegant young dandy as a figurehead on the throne, she quietly pushed him aside, doing all the ruling herself, directing, planning, organizing, and ignoring her husband, Thutmose, who was far too mild and gentle to cope with the strong, virile energy that moved Hatshepsut, the Queen. Indeed, Hat-

Thutmose I declares his young daughter Hatshepsut his successor on the throne of Egypt. His son, Thutmose II, thus cut off from his inheritance, stands by in impotent dismay, while the crowd of courtiers rejoices.

shepsut asserted that she was Queen and Pharaoh by right of her father's decree, and that Thutmose was no more than a low-born interloper who had no right whatever to reign as King by her side.

In all save name, Hatshepsut was, indeed, the Pharaoh yet she could have no title except that of "Royal Wife."

Moreover, Hatshepsut's first child was a daughter named No-fru're; no son was born to the Queen. The little Princess Nofrure remained for many years Hatshepsut's only child, and she was brought up as heir to the throne, in charge of the noble Sen'mut, a faithful friend to the Queen.

But Thutmose II had other children born of other wives, and one of his sons, a third Thutmose, was a favorite with the King. Perhaps the poor Pharaoh, so snubbed and ignored, loved this young boy's mother, humble though her birth had been, far more than he loved Hatshepsut, the strong-minded, high-handed queen! However that may be, there seemed not the slightest chance that Thutmose, son

Thutmose II arranges a trick whereby the statue of A'mon, as it is carried through the temple, is made by the priests to nod its head toward the young prince Thutmose III, as if appointing him the next Pharaoh of Egypt.

of Thutmose, should ever inherit the throne of the wide-flung Egyptian empire, and so he was placed in the Temple to serve with the priests of Amon.

But when a second daughter, Hatshepsut Mer-yt're, was born to the Queen, Thutmose made up his mind to a bold and sudden stroke. He dared not oppose Hatshepsut by openly declaring his son to be his heir; but the priests of Amon favored the lad, and they arranged a trick to deceive the simple people.

There came a great religious festival at Kar'nak. The temple was gay with pennants and crowded with worshipping throngs. The statue of Amon himself was to be taken out of its holy place and borne about through the temple while the King officiated, sacrificing oxen, calves and mountain goats.

Prince Thutmose stood in the great north hall and when the priests left the sanctuary, bearing the statue of Amon through the midst of the waiting crowd, they secretly

Queen Hatshepsut as a woman with the vulture crown of a Queen. From her temple at Der el Bahri near Thebes.

made the stone image turn its face this way and that, as though it was searching for someone. As they arrived directly in front of the young Prince Thutmose, they tilted the statue toward him, as though Amon were pointing him out! The boy fell flat on his face, prostrate before the statue, and his father pretended surprise, while the priests explained to the people that Amon had chosen Thutmose III to be the next King of Egypt! Thereupon all the people hailed Thutmose as chosen heir, and he entered the Holy of Holies, where only the King might stand!

Now Hatshepsut, the Queen, was taken as much by surprise as her husband pretended to be. But against the faith of the people in the divine decree of Amon, she could do nothing at all; and when Thutmose II, soon after this, died, she could not prevent the youth from being crowned as Pharaoh; but she would not let him make good his claim by marrying one of her daughters of wholly royal birth. She refused to give him to wife Nofrure or little Hatshepsut.

Here was a boy on the throne, and Hatshepsut at thirty-five with no legal right to any power save that accorded Queen Mothers! Ambitious, strong-minded woman, she would not lay down the scepter. She caused herself to be hailed as regent of the land to reign beside Thutmose III.

The young boy Thutmose, however, was no mild, elegant

dandy. He was short and stocky and strong like his grandfather, Thutmose I, as strong indeed in his nature as the
Queen Hatshepsut herself. But he was young and un-
learned in the ways of managing men; he was only a boy of
sixteen, accounted no more than a child.

For nine years the boy tried to rule, to be Pharaoh not
merely in name, but he could not cope with Hatshepsut.

She thrust him into the shade, to live for twelve years a
nobody, a strong young man chafing bitterly, having
scarcely a show of power.

At last she persuaded the people that she, the only one
of her line of wholly royal birth, was her father's real heir,
and Thutmose the second and third, had had no legal right
to rule. She got the people to give her the lofty title of
Pharaoh, and she vigorously blotted out on temples, pillars,
and monuments the name of Thutmose II, replacing it
with the name of Thutmose I, her father.

Henceforth, Hatshepsut saw to it that she was always
addressed not as Queen, but as King, and always as His
Majesty. She came forth on state occasions clad in the
garments of a man, wearing the short kilt and sandals and
the great war-helmet of the Pharaohs, and even attaching

Hatshepsut as a man; a statue and a painting from her temple near Thebes, each showing her with the artificial
beard. The picture at the right without beard shows her wearing the great war helmet of the Pharaohs, and the
kilt of a man. A relief from Karnak. This great queen's name is also written Hatasu.

The beautiful temple of Queen Hatshepsut beneath the western cliffs of Thebes. These cliffs gleam pink or peach-colored from the distance. Close to, they look like white chalk thickly powdered with cinnamon. The temple rises in three terraces approached by an inclined plane. The shrine is cut into the solid rock on the third terrace. Before the temple were found the sunken squares of lotus pools and round holes cut in the solid rock of the desert. These holes were filled with rich dirt and in them trees were planted, so that even across the desert, this beautiful temple was approached from the Nile through a garden and avenue of trees. Behind these cliffs lies the famous Valley of the Tombs of the Kings. Across the Nile is the modern Egyptian city of Luxor.

to her chin the Pharaoh's long false beard. Thus garbed, she had herself carved and painted on all the records of stone erected during her reign.

Moreover, on inscriptions referring to herself, she mixed up *he's* and *she's* in a most remarkable way. "*His* Majesty," she announced, "gave these obelisks to *her* father."

At last, after years of struggle, Hatshepsut found herself free to rule the land alone, and she devoted all her energies to building and organizing, neglecting the Syrian wars, but increasing her country's resources with the aid of her group of nobles,—Sen'mut, now Steward of the vast estates of the Queen, Ne-he'si, soldier and sailor, and Hap'u-sonb, the Prime Minister, who was also High Priest of Amon, and thus had won the Amon priesthood over to the Queen.

And while Hatshepsut pursued with vigor all the arts of peace, her soldiers sat about idle, and the young man Thutmose III, forced into inactivity, fretted himself in secret, because he could not lead forth his hosts, as his grandfather Thutmose had done, to cement a mighty empire, perhaps to conquer the earth.

In the hills of the western desert, the queen began to build her beautiful temple and tomb, the most beautiful building Egyptian art was ever to produce. Three rows of peach-colored pillars rose up in three terraces, against the pale-gold background of a semi-circle of cliffs. A broad roadway mounted the slopes flanked by rows of sphinxes, and led up to the sanctuary cut in the solid rock.

The work was in charge of Senmut. Swarms of workmen lived there under shelters of thatch. Tourists, too, crowded the place. There were tombs in the cliffs round about, and the beautiful little tomb of one of the Men-tu-ho'teps, already seven hundred years old, was just next door to the temple. Tourists came gaping and wondering, three thousand years ago, to view those antique curiosities and scribble their names on the walls just as they do today.

Senmut himself was so proud of his work that he wanted somehow to leave himself stamped upon it forever; but only Kings and Queens were allowed to be represented praying before the gods in such a temple as this; so Senmut caused a figure of himself praying toward the altar, to be secretly carved on the inner side of every dark closet door, hoping that, with luck, he might never be discovered, but might continue throughout all time to stay there in the dark, praying toward the altar!

The Figure of Senmut, architect of the temple, hidden on the inner side of a closet door where he hoped to pray to the gods undisturbed through eternity.

Meantime while the temple was building, the Queen conceived the ambitious plan of sending an expedition by sea to bring back incense trees from the far-off land of Punt, which had been so little visited during Herdsmen days and later, that it seemed again to Egyptians to be a Land of Mystery from which they got the products only in roundabout ways, through the hands of desert-traders.

Hatshepsut gathered together five large sailing vessels, each having an upcurved stern in the shape of a lotus flower. The sailors set forth from Thebes on their long adventurous journey under command of Nehesi, facing the unknown seas with only most ancient records by which to steer their course.

Far down the African coast they sailed, singing an oarsman's chant to the rhythmic fall of the oars.

At last they turned up a river lined with conical huts which were built up high on piles and entered only by ladders. Beneath palm trees and sycamores, cattle lay on the ground, while monkeys and baboons climbed among the branches and brilliantly colored birds went flitting through the air. White dogs guarded the huts, and here and there

Huts of the natives of Punt, built up on piles and approached by ladders. They stand on the banks of a river in a grove of date palms and myrrh trees, beneath which a cow is slumbering. All the story of this voyage is taken from pictures carved on the walls of Hatshepsut's temple at Der el Bahri. For the situation of Punt, see the map, page 71.

were seen yawning hippopotami, panthers and giraffes.

This was the land of Punt and Nehesi went ashore at once, followed by a guard of soldiers, bearing gifts from the ships,—gaily colored glass beads, bracelets, daggers, axes, which they placed upon a low table, temptingly spread out. And the people came to meet him,—clean-shaven natives in kilts, the men having long, thread-like beards, curled up at the end like the beards of the gods in Egypt.

The chieftain came himself, Pir-o'hu, the Great One of Punt, and behind him came his wife, the royal lady Ati, so fat she could scarcely waddle, her fat hanging out in rolls and causing the Egyptian artist who went with Hatshepsut's sailors to smile with inward delight.

Lady Ati wore a skirt of thin, transparent yellow, not to hide too much her beautiful cushions of fat. Behind her came two sons and a daughter with upraised hands of greeting, the daughter already tending to the same fat fashion of loveliness attained by her proud mama.

In the rear of the family there followed attendants driving a donkey, loaded down with cushions, his business being to bear on his back the enormous Princess Ati; and the very small size of the donkey compared with the size of his burden, caused the artist of Egypt to chuckle once again.

The natives of Punt greet the Egyptian adventurers. The Prince of Punt followed by his fat wife, two sons and a daughter, all raise their hands in greeting. Behind them come attendants driving a very small donkey whose business, so the inscription says, is to carry the fat Lady Ati. The men of Punt have long threadlike beards curled up at the end. They wear peculiarly shaped kilts and have tails attached to their belts in the rear. The Princess Ati has lines of tattooing on her cheeks and wears a transparent yellow skirt, the better to display her cushiony limbs.

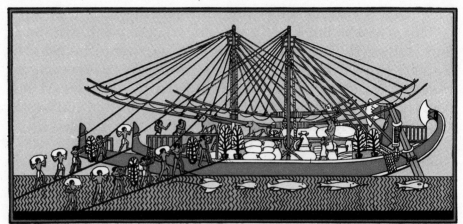

Natives of Punt loading the ships for the return voyage. Some carry bundles on their shoulders; others have myrrh-trees in baskets swung from poles which they carry on their shoulders, as they march in line up the gang planks. Myrrh-trees in baskets, with all sorts of bundles and bales, crowd the deck of the ship. Above there are apes, and over the cabin at the left, a man is teasing a monkey. The ships are moored to stakes which show at the right.

So surprised were these people of Punt to look on the sailors from Egypt, that they cried aloud to Nehesi:

"How did you come hither? Did you descend from the paths of the skies? Or did you sail over the waters?"

Friendly relations at once were established. Nehesi pitched his tent in incense groves near the sea and gave a feast to the chief, serving bread, beer, meats and fruit; and the chieftain brought him presents of gold rings, throw-sticks, and boomerangs together with a pile of precious incense gum.

The men of Punt, bearing produce of their land, are met on the shores of Egypt by a triumphal procession. The Queen's fan-bearers and her sandal-bearer head the procession with the royal symbols.

Then the ships were loaded with products of the land,—ivory, ebony, ostrich feathers, monkeys, dogs, and apes, panthers, panther-skins, giraffes, gold, silver, lapis-lazuli, natives and their children, throw-sticks and boomerangs, and living incense trees in baskets or in pits. Never was the like brought home to any king since the very beginning of history,—so the monuments said!

As the ships sailed back to Egypt, incense trees stood on the decks; monkeys and baboons went climbing about in the rigging.

Great was the welcome the sailors received when they stepped on shore again and marched up from their vessels, followed by the natives of Punt, bearing all the rich stores of their land. Men shouted till the heavens rang: "May Amon grant long life unto Hatshepsut, his daughter!"

And there came out to meet the sailors a joyous, triumphal procession,—soldiers of the royal household, bearing green boughs in their hands, priests with the sacred ark, fan-bearers holding their long-handled fans of waving ostrich feathers, grooms leading hunting leopards, and lastly, borne by twelve bearers, the royal chair of state.

Grooms lead the Queen's hunting leopards and last comes her Majesty's chair of state. The Queen herself is awaiting the procession in the Temple of Amon at Karnak across the Nile from her own temple-tomb.

The Queen in the kilt of a man and wearing the ceremonial crown of Amon with the ram's horns and feathers, waits to receive her troops in the temple of Amon.

The Queen herself had gone to the temple of Amon where she received her sailors in the costume of a Pharaoh while the natives of Punt did obeisance before her. All the rich treasures they brought, Hatshepsut presented to Amon. And her Majesty covered her limbs with the very best of the incense, till the fragrance exuding from her was like the breath of the gods.

Thereafter she held a levee, sitting in her great audience-hall on her splendid throne of electrum, while the nobles and peers of the court came to rejoice and to praise her. The precious incense trees were planted before her temple, either in tubs or in holes dug into the rock, and there they exuded sweet fragrance before her favorite gods.

And now, at last, when Hatshepsut felt herself so well established in Egypt that she no more feared the young Thutmose, she let him marry her eldest daughter, the Princess Royal, Nofrure.

In the thirtieth year of her reign she celebrated her jubilee, erecting at Karnak two obelisks, quarried from granite of A-swan', and brought downstream on a barge towed by twenty-seven boats with oars.

Thus the last years of Hatshepsut were spent in glorious splendor, in a court superior to anything ever known before in Egypt. But her fame, which spread to the ends of the world, was always a fame for peace, and not for war or conquest, a fame for wisdom in government, for development of resources, and ceaseless splendid building. The story of Hatshepsut is that of the first great woman in history.

Thutmose III, the Conqueror

(1480–1447 B. C.)

When Queen Hatshepsut died, Thutmose III, already nearly forty and growing somewhat bald, had been so long repressed that his forceful spirit, pent-up and thirsting for adventure, burst at once into flame. He had, first of all, to quell a revolt in Thebes; for Senmut and the nobles were heading an insurrection, knowing well they had nothing to hope for at the hands of Thutmose III. But Thutmose defeated the nobles and Senmut was forced to flee.

Then at last Thutmose set out with his band of eager soldiers on their much delayed journey to Syria; for Syria, so divided into small city-states, each with its own king or prince, and its own local

Head of a statue of Thutmose III, a stocky little man with a thick strong neck, a huge forceful nose, but a kindly smiling mouth. The nose and neck are those of the powerful warrior. The mouth is that of the sweet-natured man, who with boyish enthusiasm gathered the gorgeous wild flowers on the plains of Palestine and said that he preferred shy people to proud ones. The king's name is also written Thothmes or Tutmosis. This statue was found in the temple of Amon at Karnak, Thebes, and is now in the Cairo Museum.

Baal or god, for the first time in its history presented a united front. A great Asiatic confederacy, headed by the King of Ka'desh, most powerful of Syria's princes, had determined to throw off the yoke imposed on them by Thutmose I some fifty years before.

Crossing the desert quickly, Thutmose III marched up the coast, meeting little opposition till he came where the Ridge of Mt. Carmel thrusts a bold promontory into the Great

Egypt and the lands to the North which the Pharaohs attempted to conquer. The positions of the different kingdoms are certain, but their exact outlines are unknown and the colors indicate borders only in a general way. The
dotted line of long dashes — — — indicates the extent of Egyptian conquest. The land of Naharin which included part of Syria and all of the Mitanni became the northern limit of the Egyptian Empire. From these subject nations there flowed into Thebes a constant stream of tribute which made Egypt enormousy wealthy.

Green Sea. Here he came to a halt; for news was brought
to his ears that his enemy, the King of Kadesh had left
his home to the northward and marched as far south as
Megiddo where he lay encamped but a few miles away, just
over the range of hills. Moreover, the princes of an hundred
confederate Syrian states had gathered at Me-gid'do to con-
sult with the King of Kadesh, but they had not brought
their troops; for they had never even dreamed that Thutmose would act so quickly. If Thutmose could take Megiddo, he would catch all his foes at once.

Immediately the great Pharaoh summoned his council of
war to decide by which of three routes they should cross the
ridge of Carmel. The safest road lay by Ta'a-nach; the most
direct but most dangerous went by way of Aruna, descend-

ing straight on Megiddo, but this road led through a pass, so very narrow and dangerous that men must march through it single-file and could never have formed in battle array had the enemy fallen upon them.

"We go by the pass!" ordered Thutmose.

But his officers said in terror: "Let our victorious lord march by the road he wishes, but let him not oblige us to go by that most perilous route."

"As the Sun-god loves me!" cried Thutmose; "as my father Amon favors me, I swear my Majesty will march by none other road save this! Let him among you who wishes, go by the roads you have mentioned; and let him among you who wishes come with those who follow my Majesty!"

At this the generals gave up. "We will follow your Majesty," they said, "like the servant behind his master."

Then his Majesty swore a round oath. "None shall march on this road in front of my Majesty!" he cried.

And he himself led the way. Like a flame of fire was the King. He marched at the head of his army.

Now the King of Kadesh was expecting Thutmose by

the safest route through Taanach; so, accompanied by the Prince of Megiddo in numerous battle array, he left the other princes shut up in Megiddo and camped in front of Taanach, settling himself at ease in his splendid campaigning tent which had tent-poles wrought with silver.

Then suddenly out of the rocky defile, Thutmose appeared with his army, throwing his forces between the unfortunate King of Kadesh and those wretched allied princes whom he had left in Megiddo.

Standing upon the walls and straining their eyes in the darkness, the princes saw with terror the myriad lights of Pharaoh's camp between them and their protector who could not now come through to them without fighting all Pharaoh's host.

Next morning Thutmose arose, like to the Hawk-god, the Smiter, and he came forth in his chariot, armed with his weapons of war, to charge the King of Kadesh.

Placing himself as the striking head of a sweeping crescent of soldiers, he charged at full speed down hill, his fierce Negro troops like black giants, supported by disciplined archers and shouting charioteers.

When the untrained troops of Kadesh saw that well-ordered charge, they fled in headlong rout across the plain of Es'drae-lon till they came to the river Ki'shan, where they threw themselves into the water, abandoning horses and chariots and casting aside their armor that they might be able to swim.

Then the wings of the Egyptian army, seeing the rout of the enemy, came running up to the center to join in gathering the plunder, thus leaving the way to Megiddo free; so that some of the wretched enemy were able to make their way back as far as the city walls.

But the people inside of Megiddo, fearing to open the

The wretched kings of Megiddo and Kadesh are dragged up over the walls. The princes shut up in Megiddo were
rulers of many cities later known in the Bible. This campaign into Palestine was a campaign in Bible lands where
the native Canaanites dwelt undisturbed as yet by the Hebrews.   Megiddo is being excavated by scholars today.

gates, let down strips of twisted clothing to haul the fugitives up. The miserable King of Kadesh and the miserable Prince of Megiddo were thus hauled up in haste.

The Egyptians captured horses, armor, weapons, and even rich chariots plated with gold, together with living prisoners and the tent of the King of Kadesh with its tent-poles wrought in silver. And all the army made festival, giving thanks to Amon. But Thutmose rebuked their rejoicings.

"If you had captured the city," he cried, "I should give greater thanks! For the prince of every rebellious state is there inside that city."

And he went back at once to Megiddo, laid siege to the city and took it, so the princes came before him, begging for their lives. Then Thutmose granted them pardon, and made them vassals of his throne; for the heart of the rugged

Kneeling figures of Pharaoh's conquered foes. The black men are Nubians with ostrich feathers in their hair, bead necklaces, breast-bands with panther tails, armlets and ear-rings. The bearded man with the shawl at the left is a white man from Mitanni, the kingdom of grain-lands in the bend of the Euphrates. (See p. 197 and Vol. II, p. 51.) The bearded man at the right is a Syrian. This picture was a painting on a king's throne found near Thebes.

warrior was gentle enough at bottom. He had no wish to be cruel. If he had the fighting spirit of his grandfather, Thutmose I, he had none of that vengeful wrath which loaded captives with chains, or hung their dead bodies upside down at the masts of victorious ships.

He ordered that the sons of these princes, rulers of many cities later known in the Bible, should be sent to Egypt as hostages, to be trained in Egyptian customs; and the princes came bearing him gifts, — silver, gold and jewels; grain and wine and cattle.

But when Thutmose had taken Megiddo, he found that the King of Kadesh had already slipped away and made good his escape, and he heard that all the King's family lay encamped on the slopes of Mt. Lebanon.

So Thutmose went forward again and attacked the camp of the King, taking captive his eighty-seven children, his wives with all their jewels, his officers and servants, together with his clothing, all his household goods, his dishes, chairs and tables, and his statue of ebony wrought with gold and inlaid with lapis-lazuli. Thus the unfortunate King who had headed the uprising returned with only the clothes on his back to his native city of Kadesh.

Having now at one bold stroke brought all Syria under

his rule, Thutmose returned to Egypt, where he celebrated his victory with sacrifices to Amon. News of his great achievement spread to the ends of the earth, so that even the King of Assyria thought best to send him a present.

When Spring of the next year came, Thutmose set forth again to visit his Syrian vassals; but this time he went not so much for war as to make a great show of his soldiers that there might be no thought of rebellion anywhere in the land. Being now less filled with thoughts of war and more able to look about him, he was struck with admiration for the beauty of the wild flowers, blue lupine and red anemones, streaking the hills and plains. With boyish enthusiasm, the sturdy, middle-aged warrior made a collection of wild flowers, that they might be transplanted to Egypt and grow in the gardens at Karnak, and he had a catalogue of the flowers carved on the temple walls.

Thenceforward Thutmose made a journey every year to

General Am-en-em'heb saves King Thutmose from a ferocious elephant as he hunts along the Euphrates near Niy.

Syria, save for those years when he celebrated the jubilee anniversaries of his coronation as Pharaoh.

Every spring for sixteen years, he either marched up northward or went in his ships by sea, displaying his forces, marching against any town that rebelled, receiving presents and collecting tribute.

Meantime the sons of the Syrian princes were being brought up in Egypt and when the former ruler died, one of these youths was sent home, trained in Egyptian culture, to govern the land of his fathers. Thutmose dreamed indeed of a peaceful, united Syria, well governed and contented under Egyptian rule.

It was not till his sixth expedition that he finally conquered Kadesh, but following his usual custom, he pardoned his stubborn, old enemy; and the King of Kadesh came unbound before his long-hated foe.

Later, Thutmose set out to surpass his grandfather's record, pushing up through the land of Na-har'in till he came to the river Euphrates where Egyptian soldiers had not been seen for fifty years at least.

On the near side of the stream, he found the triumphal tablet set up by Thutmose I and next it he placed his own.

Then he pushed on further still. He went up as far north as Carchemish on the borders of the Hittite Empire, whose rugged mountaineers would soon be Egypt's strongest foes.

There he fought a battle with the white-faced King of Mi-tan'ni, an Aryan king of the land, who had long opposed him unpunished. He scattered the hosts of Mitanni, —"not one looked behind him; but they fled away, forsooth, like a flock of mountain goats!"

Thus Thutmose was able at last to cross the river Euphrates and set up his boundary stone on the eastern bank of the stream, an achievement which he had striven for ten long years to attain.

At Niy, Thutmose settled down no more than a few hundred miles from Carchemish and Babylon, and there he hunted the elephants among the rocks of the river, nearly losing his life when one ferocious elephant whom he had attacked single-handed, turned and charged him madly. His general Am-en-em'hab saved his life on that hunt by cutting off the elephant's trunk.

Unto Niy came messengers bearing to Thutmose tribute from the recently conquered princes. Moreover the King of Babylon and the King of the Hittites likewise sent splendid presents to Thutmose.

In his sixteenth and last campaign, Thutmose conquered the last Syrian prince who had managed to hold out against him, the stiff-necked Prince of Tunip. Thus when his yearly visits ceased, Syria, so unruly, so filled with rebellious princelings, was at last subdued.

In gratitude for his victories, Thutmose built at Karnak, amid that imposing collection of temples constructed by different Pharaohs, a splendid temple to Amon, having pillars like tent-poles, its hall like a great tent in stone; for he thought of Amon as a god of war, ever giving him victory and more at home in a campaigning tent than in a house or shrine. Here at Karnak he caused his great Hymn of Victory to be inscribed. Thus said the powerful Amon-ra, unto the Pharaoh Thutmose:

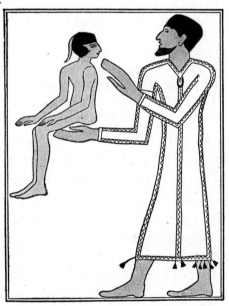

The Prince of Tunip offers one of his children to Pharaoh. The naked little child has the "lock of infancy" hanging down behind. From the tomb of Men-kheper-re-seneb in western Thebes.

The god Amon from whose head rise the two imposing feathers of truth, bestows imperial power on Thutmose III.
Amon, in early days an unimportant tribal god of Thebes, gradually gained in importance as Thebes became the
ruling city in Egypt. The fighting Pharaohs of the 18th Dynasty, whose family came from Thebes, made their
great war-god Amon greater than Ra and Osiris, the chief god of all the land, and they called him Amon-ra.

"I have given you dominion and victory over all countries;
I have come causing you to strike at the princes of Syria;
I have hurled them beneath your feet among the highlands,
I have come causing you to strike at the lands of the West;
Crete and Cyprus are in panic;
The lands of Mitanni tremble in fear of you;
I have made them see your Majesty as a crocodile,
Lord of the terror that is in the water, the unapproachable one.
I have come causing you to strike at the Libyans;
I have made them see your Majesty as a fierce-eyed lion.
The arms of my Majesty are above you warding off evil;
And I have caused you to reign, my beloved son."

But for all the warlike note sounded by this hymn, Thutmose, the collector of wild-flowers, was at heart a lovable
fellow, a plain, straight-forward warrior, who fed and
pardoned his enemies and publicly recorded that "he loved
shy-ones better than proud."

The only foe whom he never forgave was his high-handed
aunt, Hatshepsut, she who had kept him in eclipse all the best
years of his life; for when Hatshepsut's memory began to fade
in the hearts of his people, he ordered her statues smashed,
and wiped out so far as he could all mention of her name,
replacing it with the name of Thutmose II, his father.

This one act of vengeance remains the only blot on the name of Thutmose III, the greatest warrior of Egypt, who ruled a larger empire than any other Pharaoh.

A joyous city was Thebes in the days of Pharaoh Thutmose. City of an hundred gates, it lay between tall cliffs at the very edge of the desert.

On the eastern bank rose the palace of the Pharaohs, the houses of nobles and citizens and the mighty collection of temples built by the Pharaohs at Karnak. Amid the crowds on the streets appeared ambassadors from foreign kings, Cretans in loin-cloths and tight jewelled belts; Negroes in feather head-dresses, Syrians swathed in gay-colored wool and Libyans from the desert. In the markets

A street in Thebes in the days of Thutmose III. To the left the house has columns with capitals shaped like palm leaves; the next house has columns with capitals like the lotus-flower and the lotus buds which the girl in the foreground carries in her hands. The third house has columns with capitals like the papyrus flower which appears to grow up from a cluster of leaves. The man in the foreground is carrying on his back a bundle of real papyrus reeds for the making of paper. The temple to the right has capitals with heads of the goddess Hathor, showing her quaint cow's ears. These were the chief forms of capitals in Egyptian architecture. See page 115.

Passing in the street are people from the subject nations of the now mighty Empire: Asiatics, Libyans, Negroes, with friendly visitors from the Island of Crete.

Daily life in the fields in the days of Thutmose III. At the left a man with a sickle is cutting the grain, which other men carry away in a basket slung on a pole. Nearby, two quarrelsome girls engage in a hair-pulling contest, men rest in the shade of a tree and an overseer, standing at ease as he leans upon his staff, watches men heap up the grain.

produce from the farm-lands was brought in on little donkeys attended by gaping countrymen, fresh from the cutting, the threshing, or the winnowing of grain.

On the river passed gaily painted barks; on the streets were triumphal processions, or pageants of the gods, marching to the temples or over the river to the City of the Dead and the desolate valley of glistening white cliffs, streaked as with powdered cinnamon, where the Tombs of the Kings were hidden amid the sands of the desert.

Life was gay and busy in the swarming city of Thebes.

Oxen thresh out the heads of the wheat by patiently treading upon it. Nearby men winnow the wheat, tossing it up in the air till the chaff is blown away and the golden kernels, freed from the chaff, fall in a heap on the ground. These scenes are from the tomb of Menna in Thebes. Menna was a superintendent of the estates of the king and of Amon in the middle of the 18th dynasty.

Banquet guests and 3 dancing girls from the 18th dynasty tomb of Nakht at Thebes. The women are dressed in their best; a gay fillet binds their wigs and holds a lotus blossom which droops coquettishly over the eyes. In the ears are round ear-rings and around the neck are collars. On their heads are cakes of perfume which gradually melt.

There were laughter, dancing and music, wreaths and garlands of flowers. The very names of the children were gay and sweet and tender,—Eyes-of-Love, and My-Lady-Is-as-Gold, they called little girls in those days, Beautiful-Morning, Little-wild Lion, I-Have-Wanted-You, and Sweetheart.

And the people drew funny pictures even on the walls of their tombs. They might be very solemn on state religious occasions, but at other times they laughed—they dearly loved to laugh. They laughed at pictures of animals performing ridiculous antics,—wolves parading with goats, or the King of the Mice in a chariot attacking a troop of cats!

A proud rat, carrying a nose-gay, and about to drink from a festive bowl, her head crowned with a lotus flower, her tail proudly trailing behind, is waited upon by a sad-looking cat carrying a fan and a napkin. Between the two lies a trussed goose. (New York Historical Society.) At the right is the most ancient version of a pussy-cat under her mistress' chair as in our own nursery rhyme of *Pussy Cat, Pussy Cat, where have you been?* (Tomb of Nakht, Thebes.)

A comic strip from a papyrus in the British Museum. A cat with a crooked stick drives a flock of geese. A wolf with a staff and knapsack parades with a herd of goats while a second wolf playing the pipes, merrily brings up the rear.

And the old warriors told large tales concerning incidents that had occurred in the various campaigns in Syria.

Some old soldier originating a tale that was later to become the story of Ali Baba, would tell how General Thutiy took the city of Joppa by hiding men in jars which he loaded on the backs of asses and drove in sight of the foe; so the Prince of Joppa, sore-hungered, seized the caravan and took it inside the walls, where the hidden soldiers sprang forth and captured the astonished city.

Other tales too the old warriors told concerning far-away lands, stories curiously like the fairy tales of today. One of these dealt with Na-har'in, that farthest land to the northward ever subdued by Thutmose. The name of this story was:

The King of the Mice attacks the Cats in a chariot drawn by dogs. His bold mouse-warriors advance in good order behind their shields; one scales the ladder to the fortress while the cats in great dismay prance wildly in the field or raise their paws in alarm atop their threatened walls. (Erman, Adolf: *Life in Ancient Egypt.*)

The Story of the Prince and the Three Dooms*

There was once a King of Egypt to whom no son was born; and he prayed the gods for a child. And his wife brought forth a son.

Then came the Hathors, goddesses who decree for children a destiny. And the Hathors said, "This child will die either by a crocodile, a serpent, or a dog."

So his Majesty's heart was sickened and he caused a house to be built in the desert. It was furnished with all good things that the child should not go abroad.

But the child went up on the roof, and he saw a dog, following after a man who was walking on the road below.

And the child said to his servant: "What is that that follows after the man?"

And the servant answered: "That is a dog."

And the child said: "Bring me such an one."

Then the servant told his Majesty. And his Majesty said, "Bring the boy a little pet dog, lest his heart be sad."

And behold they brought him the dog.

And when the child was grown, he sent to his father

*This story is given in "Egyptian Tales" second series, by W. M. Flinders Petrie.

saying: "Wherefore am I kept here? If I am doomed to three evil fates, let me go forth and meet them."

So they took him to the east country, and said: "Behold, go whither thou wilt."

His dog was with him, and he went northward, following his heart in the desert, while he lived on the best of the game. He went to the chieftain of Naharin.

And behold, there had not been born to the chieftain of Naharin any child save a daughter. Behold, there had been built for her a house; its seventy windows were seventy cubits from the ground.

And the chieftain caused to be brought all the sons of the chiefs of Shalu, and he said unto them: "Whosoever reaches the window of my daughter, she shall be to him for a wife."

And many days after this, as the princes were gathered together, the youth came riding by. The princes took him to their house, they bathed him, they perfumed him, they gave him portions of their own food, and they said, "Whence comest thou, goodly youth?"

He said to them, "I am son of an officer from Egypt, fleeing from my stepmother. But tell me, what do ye here?"

They answered him: "We climb; for he who shall reach the window of the Princess of Naharin, to him she shall be for a wife."

And the youth said: "Let me behold this."

So they went to climb as aforetime. And the youth stood far off to behold, but the Princess turned her face towards him.

And the next day the youth came likewise to climb with the sons of the chiefs.

He climbed, and he reached the window. The Princess of Naharin kissed him; she embraced him.

And one told her father, saying: "Lo, one of the youths hath reached thy daughter's window!"

The Princess of Naharin was white-skinned in contrast to the reddish skin of the Egyptians. She was a Princess of the Mitanni, that far northern Asiatic country which Thutmose conquered (see page 188 and map 182). Amenhotep III had a Mitannian princess as one of his wives, and the Pharaohs who followed him frequently took wives from the various tribes of Asia. (See illustrations page 186 and also Vol. II, page 51.)

And the Chief said: "Which of the princes is it?"

And the messenger replied: " 'Tis the son of an officer from Egypt who is fleeing from before his stepmother."

Then the Chief was angry and cried: "Shall I give my daughter to a fugitive? Let him go back whence he came!"

And one went to tell the youth. But the maiden seized his hand; she swore an oath by Ra, saying, "By the being of Ra Ho-rakh'ti, if one takes him from me, I will not eat, I will not drink, I shall die in that same hour."

Then the chieftain sent men to slay the youth, while he was in his house. But the maiden said, "By the being of Ra, if one slay him, I shall be dead ere the sun goeth down."

So the Chief gave the youth his daughter to wife. He gave him also a house, and slaves, and fields; also cattle, and all manner of good things.

But the youth said to his wife: "I am doomed to die either by a crocodile, a serpent, or a dog."

And the wife feared greatly for her husband, and would not let him go abroad alone.

And they set out together toward Egypt.

Behold the crocodile of the river, he came out by the town in which the youth was. And a giant of the town kept the crocodile bound and when the giant walked out of the house he led the crocodile and the crocodile walked behind.

Now when evening came, the youth lay down on his bed. Sleep seized upon his limbs.

Then came a serpent from his hole, to bite the youth. Behold, his wife was sitting by him; she lay not down.

Thereupon the servants gave milk to the serpent, and the serpent drank, and was drunk, and lay upside down. And the Prince's wife made the serpent to perish with the blows of her dagger.

And the youth awoke, astonished. And his wife said unto him: "Behold, thy god hath saved thee from one of thy dooms. He will also save thee from the others."

And the youth sacrificed to Ra, adoring him.

And when the days were passed after these things, the youth went to walk in the fields. He went not alone; behold, his dog was following him. And his dog ran aside after the wild game, and he followed the dog. He came to the river, and entered the river behind his dog.

Then came the crocodile, and seized the Prince and carried him off to the giant. And the crocodile said:

"I am thy doom following after thee!"*

But the dog fell on the crocodile and killed him.

Then the giant fell on the Prince, the struggle was sore, and the dog fell on the giant and they rolled together in an

*Here the papyrus of this very interesting old fairy tale is destroyed. The ending is the editor's addition, worked out as the ending was evidently prepared for in the earlier part of the story.

heap. None knew which was the limb of the giant and which was the limb of the Prince.

And the dog slew the giant; but in the confusion of struggle he bit his master likewise; the Prince was like to die.

And the dog mourned and would not eat and the Princess mourned and said: "Alack, that he who loved the Prince should carry out the doom!"

And she called on the name of Ra, and Ra heard her prayer, and the Prince returned to health and the dog licked his hand in joy. And the Princess said:

"Behold thy god hath saved thee from all thy dooms."

And the youth sacrificed to Ra, adoring him.

Then the youth said to the Princess: "Behold, I am not the son of a fugitive, but the son of Pharaoh himself!"

And he took her hand and led her to Pharaoh.

And Pharaoh rejoiced to see his son and the wife he had brought from Naharin.

And it came to pass in process of time that they two sat on the throne as King and Queen of Egypt.

A typical representation of a Pharaoh of the Empire holding subject nations, apparently Asiatics, by the hair of their heads while a goddess leads a list of conquered cities. From a bas-relief in one of the temples of Karnak.

The First Great Adventure in Thinking

AKHNATON (Ok-nah'tun) 1375–1350 B. C.

Amen-ho'tep II, who followed Thutmose III was far more fierce than his father. A man of enormous strength, he could draw a bow which none of his soldiers could bend, and he led his armies into the newly-won countries of Asia, merciless, proud and cruel. Into the harbor of Thebes he

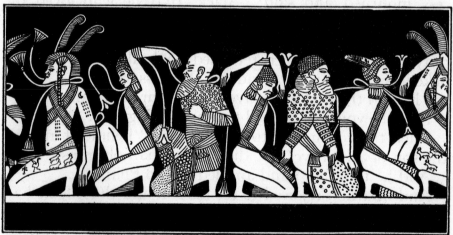

Two Libyans, three Negroes and two Asiatics bound with lotus and papyrus flowers as a symbol of their subjection to the mighty Egyptian Empire. Note the tattooing and peculiar head-dress of the Libyans. These pictures are exquisitely wrought on the gold plating that covered the chariot of Tut-ankh-amen. Cairo Museum.

Scribes count hands of the slain and officers lead Libyan prisoners manacled in painful positions before a Pharaoh of the Empire. Typical of the stern warfare of the fighting Pharaohs. Temple of Ramses III, Medinet Habou.

sailed, displaying seven Syrian kings hanging head downwards from the prow of his great war-galley. Six of these he sacrificed with his own hands on the bloody altar of Amon; the seventh he carried off to a far-away city of Nubia and there hung on a gateway as a ghastly warning to all rebel chiefs.

Amenhotep II was followed by his son, Thutmose IV, and his grandson, Amenhotep III, a lazy, indolent man who dwelt in such brilliant splendor that he was called the Magnificent.

Now unto this king was born a son, called Amenhotep the fourth. The boy was a dreamy child, thoughtful and serious-eyed, yet full of an inner fire. In the palace at the edge of the desert he raced through halls of columns and over painted pavements where wild ducks swam amid lotus flowers, while on the ceiling above him painted pigeons flew, white against a blue sky. Through curtained doorways, he peeped out on sun-lit gardens or on the pillared balcony, where his father and mother sat to receive queer foreign ambassadors together with stores of tribute from all the far ends of the empire. Here the boy saw banquets, jubilee celebrations and festivals on the water, dazzling in brilliance and splendor.

Queen Tiy called her splendid barge *Aton-gleams*. The setting sun in Egypt was called Atum, a word probably connected with the Syrian-Hebrew word Adon which is still used to mean Lord God. Queen Tiy was part Asiatic. Though she wore a black wig, her hair was not black like the Egyptians but red like the Syrians, as shown by a lock found in the tomb of Tut-ankh-amen, her grand-daughter's husband. Through his father, also, Akhnaton was part Asiatic, related to the Hebrews; for Amenhotep III was son of a Mitannian Princess. In this picture Queen Tiy wears around her neck a quaint little crouching gold figure of her husband, found in the tomb of Tut-ankh-amen.

On the eastern side of the palace Amenhotep III had dug a pleasure lake to amuse his auburn-haired queen, Tiy, the Great Royal Wife. On this shining body of water, the Queen and her son often floated, the boy at his mother's feet, as they sat in their golden barge looking westward over the sands to the splendid cliffs of Thebes, pink and golden in sunlight, blue and lilac in shadow.

But in this world of beauty the child was always wondering, persistently asking those questions that children always ask, yet not content to be turned aside with foolish, inadequate answers, like those the priests of Amon doled out to quiet little boys.

"What gives the little chick life?" he asked, "and makes him chirp and run about when he pecks his way out of the shell? What makes the lambs skip, the butterflies fly, the birds flit about in the marshes?"

Trickery and deceit had long characterized the domineering priesthood of Amon, whose power over the minds of men this child Amenhotep IV, and his mother Queen Tiy so persistently challenged with their questions.

According to Mr. Wm. Reavell in the Illustrated London News, the priests tricked their people by fake miracles such as causing temple doors to open mysteriously without the help of hands. In this picture air inside an altar is expanded by heat and drives water from the round vessel below into the bucket. The added weight of the water causes the bucket to sink and thus pulls a rope connected with the door posts. Mysteriously the doors open and the image of Amon appears. All this apparatus, Mr. Reavell says, was hidden beneath the floor.

Thus he forever questioned, his eager intelligence pressing unceasingly toward an answer. Here was a boy whom the priests could not trick with all their clever deceits, one whose questions the wise men could not satisfy with all their colorful myths so appealing to childish fancy. His thoughts were always active, his heart was always tender.

Naught did he know of the savagery of Amenhotep II or of the lazy magnificence of Amenhotep III. He delighted to walk in the gardens, to hear the birds sing, to follow the butterflies, but first, last and always, he thought, he reasoned, he questioned, breaking through old superstitions, clear-eyed and knowing no fear. Already, small boy though he was, his people called him Lord of the Breath of Sweetness, and they loved him with all their hearts.

Now the great Queen Tiy, the boy's mother, made no attempt whatever to satisfy his questions with any silly evasions. She, too, pondered the matter and never tired of talking with him in sensible, reasonable fashion, as though he had been a man. Thus the two slowly worked out for themselves what it was they really believed about how the world had life.

It was no cow-headed, hippopotamus-headed monster who gave life to chicks and lambs, to birds and butterflies.

It was not that ram-headed creature Khnum who lived in the caves near the First Cataract and was forever molding Nile mud into men and women, as some good people said.

It was not even Amon who had supplanted Ra as chief of the gods of Egypt, Amon the fierce and vengeful, the god of battles and bloodshed, to whom the Egyptians prayed when they clubbed the heads of their enemies or hung them up by their heels. Amon gave death not life.

The Giver of Life was a Power unseen, tender, intelligent, loving, one of whom no pictures, no statues could be made, because he was Life itself, the life that all living beings expressed in action, intelligence, joy. This conception of God, they called Aton or Lord, and they knew no outward sign by which to represent Him, save by the disk of the sun from which radiated hands as if giving life to the world; for they said to one another: "All life shines forth from the Aton, even as beams of light shine forth from the sun."

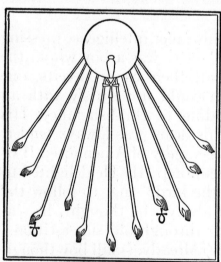

Aton or God, represented by the sign of the sun disk from which radiate rays that end in little hands very tenderly bestowing the ankh ☥ or sign of life on the world. At first Akhnaton ☥ did not know how to express his conception of a God of whom he could make no picture. The use of this sign, as well as a full understanding of his religion, was a gradual growth with Akhnaton.

And when love, warm and tender, shone in the heart of

the boy, the mother said to her son: "The Aton shines in thine heart."

Beside the Aton there was no other god at all—so mother and son came to see as they talked side by side on their golden barge, floating upon the lake, or wandered together in earnest talk amid the paths of the gardens.

Now the boy was still less than twelve when according to regular custom, a young girl was brought to the palace to be the prince's wife. Nefertiti (Nef-er-tee'tee) the child was called and she was a lovely creature, slender as a young antelope, her little head proudly poised on a long and graceful neck, her eyes somewhat dreamy and slanting, her lips very tender and full.

Henceforth there were three at the counsels, three talking and chatting together aboard the golden barge afloat on the shining lake, the young Prince Amenhotep, Nefertiti, his wife, and the Royal Mother, Queen Tiy.

Scarcely were celebrations for the boy's twelfth birthday past, when Amenhotep, his father, died in the palace at Thebes. The young boy Amenhotep and his girl-wife Nefertiti found themselves king and queen on the ancient throne of the Pharaohs with Queen Tiy to give them advice.

How full of fire was the boy! He burned with all the enthusiasm of vigorous, confident youth. He would proclaim to his people the truths which he and his mother had found concerning the true God, Aton. He would set free the thoughts of men from all those dark superstitions that hampered and bound them down with fear and dread of their gods. He would show them a God of sunshine, of gentleness and love, a merciful father and mother, who watched over all his creation with tender, compassionate care. And he thought, in his childish ignorance, that his people would welcome his vision and take it to their hearts.

Amenhotep III borne to his tomb across the river from Thebes in the Valley of the Tombs of the Kings.

Accordingly, he announced Aton to be the true God and himself to be his High Priest; he appointed as his Prime Minister a man who had not the honor of being the High Priest of Amon, and he did this in spite of the fact that for many generations none had held the high post of Prime Minister of Egypt, save the chief of the priests of Amon, that arrogant, powerful priesthood whom even the Pharaohs feared.

Who but a boy would have dared so much, who but one youthful enough to disdain all opposition because he had not yet been called upon to fight for the truths he knew? Many a Pharaoh had secretly longed to strike a blow at that priesthood, but none before this boy had ever actually dared.

The priesthood of Amon was thunder-struck, aroused, enraged, amazed! A boy to flout them thus! To preach a

To the left the beautiful young Queen Nefertiti. A painted limestone bust. The sweetness of the mouth, the fineness of the features, the long graceful neck and the poise of the chin make this one of the loveliest things ever discovered in Egypt. To the right a portrait bust of Akhnaton as a young man also showing great sweetness in the mouth and expression. Both busts were found at El Amarna. Berlin Museum.

new god of love to supplant the great god Amon, Lord of Blood and Battles! The prestige, the power of that time-honored priesthood was threatened. Religion should not come out of the dark and into the glorious sunshine! They throve on the fears, and ignorances, and blind superstitions of men.

Slowly the boy came to see that his people were not so ready as he had expected they would be, to take to their hearts the truths that seemed so simple to him. Every day he himself perfected his religion, seeing it more in its fullness, purging it of mistakes; but only a few of the nobles, grown restive under the stern demands of the ancient priesthood of Amon, hearkened with open mind to the truths concerning the Aton; the mass of people still loved their cow-headed, hawk-headed monsters. They did not wish to part with Osiris,

Bes, the merry dwarf, god of music and dancing, was the special protector of children and studied to amuse them.

Isis and Horus,—and Bes, that jolly little dwarf, the god of mirth and laughter, they would not give him up.

This god whom Amenhotep preached, —they were not allowed to picture him! And if they could not picture him, how were they to love him? This Aton never appeared as a man, and sat with men at their hearthsides to watch the kettle boil. He was not even like Ra, the sun, whom they could see in the sky. Aton was a God for whom the sun in its shining warmth was but an outward sign, a God to be seen only in all the life and joy that made the lambs to skip, the little birds to fly. Aton demanded no gorgeous show, no hecatombs of rams and bulls in bloody sacrifice; he only asked that men should live together peacefully in kindliness and love. They could not understand it! It was too simple to grasp.

Of course, the young king himself, like all the Pharaohs before him, was held to be half a god. The people venerated him and tried to understand. But even as they pretended to worship his loving Aton, they cast fearful glances about, lest some cat-headed monster should loom up in the dark to devour them for breaking their faith with Egypt's ancient gods, nor did the priesthood of Amon neglect to send subtle reports abroad to magnify all these fears.

Amenhotep grew older. He saw that his religion was not to be established without a mighty struggle, a struggle not with swords of bronze, a battle not with men; a struggle against superstitions, a mighty battle with fears. He offered men freedom, peace and life; but fighting him in the darkness was ever the priesthood of Amon!

Very well, Amenhotep settled down to fight the priest-

To the left are a row of goats drawn in the old-fashioned time-honored style acceptable to the priests, each goat walking sedately, exactly like every other with no individuality whatever; to the right are goats set free by the courage of Akhnaton. His artists drew goats full of life skipping, startled, inquisitive or shy, each having distinctly an individuality of its own.

hood of Amon, and in the realm of ideas where they had so tyrannically governed the minds of men.

The first blow he struck was at the oppressive despotism with which the priesthood had heretofore decreed the forms of art. From time immemorial, the priests had been satisfied only with paintings that showed no dangerous, individual power of thinking, to threaten their domination over the kingdom of thought. Few artists had dared to paint men except in those stiff, unlifelike, formal, dignified poses ordained by the priests of Egypt.

But the young king, now fifteen years old, gathered artists and sculptors around him and bade them show people as they were, swinging along at a walk, eating their dinner with gusto or sitting in a chair, lazily sprawled and at ease. He even ordered them to paint him kissing his pretty girl-wife of whom he was very fond!

Moreover, anxious in every way to depart from the stupid, monotonous mold with which the priests had stamped out all original inspiration, he let his artists draw caricatures, men with huge stomachs and hips, and skulls impossibly long,—anything to be different, to come out of those priestly molds, to show that men thought for themselves.

Akhnaton, leaning at ease on his staff, receives flowers from his queen. The accentuated size of stomach and hips is characteristic of this period of art when the artist was determined to do something different from the old established rule even though he made a ridiculous distortion of the human figure. Berlin Museum. A relief from El Amarna.

Thus the young king hammered boldly at the time-honored power of Amon, and sought to free the thoughts of men from its cramping, stubborn grip.

So full of fire was the boy, that he would more than once have come to an open quarrel with the priests had not his mother, Queen Tiy, gently held him back. But when his eighteenth birthday was past, even the great Queen Tiy could no longer restrain her son.

In Thebes he felt thwarted at every turn. How could he teach his people the truth of the loving Aton, the father and mother of man, when from the walls of temples, from pylons, pillars and gateways, the figure of Amon defied him? He would leave Thebes altogether. He would shake its dust forever from the soles of his gilded sandals. He would sail down the Nile, find a suitable spot and build another great city. Let the priesthood of Amon have Thebes! In his new and beautiful city he would worship his God as he chose!

Accordingly he proclaimed that he would no longer bear the name of Amen-hotep which meant the "Peace of Amon." Henceforth, let men call him Akh-naton signifying "The Glory of Aton." Then the young Akhnaton imperiously set sail down the Nile till he came to El-Amarna, 160 miles above the ancient Memphis, and there he built his new city,—palaces, gardens, shady streets, houses for common people, and a temple to Aton with broad, pillared courts, ever open to sunshine.

For two years he planned and dreamed, he oversaw, gave commands, while the city rose with marvelous speed as though he had been a wizard who had but to speak the word to turn his city of dreams into buildings of brick and stone.

When at last the city was finished, he took his beautiful wife and his three lively little daughters and floated down the Nile followed by crowds of retainers, to take up his residence at last in the city of the Horizon of Aton, there to teach and to live the religion that was his life.

In the courts of his new palace the King lived simply now, except for the great state ceremonies, and he was always happiest when his little girls frolicked about him, and his wife was by his side. "Mistress of the King's happiness," he called his wife, Nefertiti, "Lady of grace, fair of face."

To his subjects he showed himself, not as an awful Pha-

Akhnaton and Nefertiti play with their little daughters. Figures from a stela found at El Amarna. Cairo Museum.

Akhnaton and Nefertiti entertain Queen Tiy at El Amarna. The grandmother hands a choice tidbit to one little grand-daughter while Nefertiti daintily eats a roast fowl with her fingers. Akhnaton's name is also written Ikhnaton.

raoh, descendant of the gods, but as a man like themselves.

Through the streets he drove his own chariot, talking and laughing with his wife, guiding the prancing horses, and not only permitting one of his mischievous little daughters to poke a stick at his steeds, but actually ordering an artist to paint them in this position to be seen on stone for all time. Indeed, he often appeared in public holding his wife by the hand or dandling one of his babes, and he taught his people to live as honestly, as purely and as lovingly as he.

Akhnaton and Nefertiti ride abroad in their chariot, while their mischievous little daughter pokes the horses with a stick. Passers in the street make obeisance before the royal couple, and above them is the sign of Aton.

The royal family visit the temple, preceded by soldiers. Negro, Asiatic, and Libyan troopers are followed by Egyptian standard bearers and soldiers. Behind the royal couple come the little princesses, their charioteers seated in low attachments at the sides of the chariots. Above, ladies-in-waiting leave the royal palace. (From El Amarna.)

In his sunny new temple to Aton, wherein was no darkness whatever, he fearlessly worshipped his god with the simplest of ceremonies. And he wrote this hymn to Aton:

"All cattle rest upon the pastures,
  All trees and flowering things flourish,
  The birds flutter in their marshes,
  Their wings uplifted in adoration to Thee—
  All the lambs dance on their feet!
  O, Thou sole God, whose powers no other possesseth,
  Thou didst create the world according to Thy desires,
  While Thou wast alone."

Akhnaton's family worship Aton. The princesses shake their sistra before the altar; behind them come two dwarfs. The Hymn of Akhnaton, part of which is given above, resembles, in its entirety, the 104th Psalm.

And now Akhnaton had reached the height of his outward glory. Seated on a gilded double throne in a gorgeous little pavilion, he and Nefertiti received the processions of ambassadors bearing tribute from all their vast empire, while their little girls clustered about stroking a pet gazelle, and professional wrestlers and merry-makers, tumblers and graceful dancers entertained them nearby. So Akhnaton sat with his wife and his frolicsome little daughters in the last days of his happiness in the beautiful city of Aton.

Akhnaton and Nefertiti receive ambassadors from the Empire. Six little daughters stand behind their double throne. One holds a gazelle in her arms while another strokes its head. Before the royal family come two rows of Ethiopians, the men bearing bars of gold and leading leopards, the women with babies in baskets. Below is a row of Asiatics bearing a horse and chariot; for horses were brought to Egypt from Asia. Lower still are two Libyans from the Western Desert presenting ostrich eggs and feathers; behind them are two Hittites with pigtails. In the lower row behind attendants are dancers, tumblers, and wrestlers.

Akhnaton and Nefertiti carried in the state palanquin. All these pictures are from carvings at El Amarna.

The great Queen Mother died, and with her vanished the last restraint that kept the young Pharaoh from striking a crushing blow at the priesthood, who had never ceased working against him from the dismantled city of Thebes.

By imperial order, he closed the temple of Amon, he cast out its priests and ordered the name of Amon erased wherever it occurred through the length and breadth of the land.

All over Egypt his servants went, hammering the name out of temple walls, piercing their way into tombs to blot it out of texts, searching through tiny inscriptions on small statuettes and figures that the very least mention of Amon might not escape destruction.

In his eager enthusiasm, no longer kept in balance by his mother's sound good sense, the young King, so boyish still, had not the wisdom to see that blotting a name out of rocks, does not blot it out from men's hearts; he did not stop to consider that men change their thoughts very slowly, and that nothing is ever accomplished save as some truth, understood, makes over the minds of men. With all the strength of his character he hammered away at the rocks.

This is a copy of the clay letter sent by the governor of Jerusalem to Akhnaton saying, "The Khabiri are taking the cities of the King."

It was written long before the days of Moses, Joshua and the conquest of Canaan, and is one of three hundred letters found in Akhnaton's palace at El Amarna.

These Amarna letters are the oldest group of international correspondence in the world.

But now disquieting news began to drift in to the palace from far-away districts of Asia. The Hittites, a fighting people, a mongrel race of mixed tribes who lived up far to the northward, were crowding down in swarms on Egypt's possessions in Syria, and Az'i-ru, the Amorite, under pretense of protecting Akhnaton's cities in Asia against these fierce hordes of Hittites, instead, was taking them craftily, to add to his own domains.

To the eastward, the Kha-bi'ri, a Bedouin race from the desert, related perhaps to the Hebrews, raided the edge of the empire and daily took more and more land. Indeed, while Akhnaton sang hymns amid the flowers of his temple, the skies of Syria rang with songs of war and battle. All Pharaoh's far dominions found themselves of a sudden in turmoil and revolt.

"Now Tunips, thy city, weeps," wailed the loyal Governor of Tunips. "And there is no help for us."

"Let the King send troops," cried the Governor of Jerusalem; "for if no troops come this year, the whole territory of my lord, the King, will perish."

Letters poured in to the palace from all the cities of Asia. What a time it was for Akhnaton! His God was a God of peace who knew not war, nor suffering. His God was a God of love protecting all mankind, and not a mere little tribal god favoring Egypt only. Akhnaton had dreamed of an Empire held together, not by force, but by knowledge of God alone. When Aton was worshipped everywhere and his simple doctrines of love and truth were preached from every temple, then war would cease altogether and the nations would live forever at peace beneath the rule of Egypt.

And now the testing time came. Men begged him to use the sword. He had a mighty army, powerful and well trained and eager to be on the march. He had but to speak the word, to let loose upon his enemies all the hosts of destruction. Moreover, his nature was full of strength, of courage, and of fire. No warrior among his forefathers was stouter of heart than he.

But he would not fight with the sword. He fought against the sword. He wished to wipe warfare out, that love and good-will and peace might govern the nations of men. He had caught a glimpse of all men happy in mutual love and helpfulness beneath a loving God, and to make his vision prevail, he was willing to face the withering fire of opposition and hate, to be laughed at, ridiculed, scorned, by all those smaller men who would not understand.

He talked and wrote of his dreams. He tried to make peace with strong appeals sent off to the rebels in letters. But news from his frontier towns became each day sadder and sadder. The fine old soldier Ri-bad'di, the faithful King of Byblos, besieged by Bedouin foes at the foot of the hills of Lebanon, sent in a pathetic appeal.

How painful those letters were to the young and loving Akhnaton. They cut deep down to his heart, and yet he would not yield. Men should not butcher each other at any command of his. Old Am-en-ho'tep, the Conqueror, never rushed into battle with firmer determination than this great grandson displayed in refusing to go to war.

But how could the untaught people of Syria understand what moved him? They wanted nothing to do with a God who was God of all mankind. Give them a furious Baal or a blood-thirsty Teshub who favored his own people only

and boldly destroyed their foes. Moreover, what did the
people of Egypt want with a God of Peace? They loved a
God of War, who led them in their battles.

And those sturdy frontier soldiers, plain and simple of
mind, who stumbled dusty and travel-stained into the city
of Aton, bearing piteous prayers for help from the hard-
pressed princes of Syria,—they knew not what to make of it
all. The Empire was going to pieces, that mighty Empire
so gloriously won by the sword of Thutmose, the Great, yet
here was no martial music, no drum beats and blare of trum-
pets, but only a sad-eyed young Pharaoh, singing his hymns
to the Aton.

The messengers shook their heads. They longed for a
good old-fashioned sacrifice of blood, with the sensible
straightforward prayer that Amon would smite their enemies and hang them up by their heels!

At length, loyal Byblos fell, the last stronghold of that
stout old soldier, Ribaddi. Bad news followed swiftly—one
after another, Egypt's far-off fortresses fell to the power of
the foe.

And now in a frenzy, Akhnaton, suffering beyond all
endurance, determined to strike another blow at the only
foes he acknowledged. Against men he would not fight, but
to the death he would battle against men's false beliefs,
the idle gods of men's fancies. The names of every god in
the land should be erased from inscriptions, even as he had
already blotted out the name of Amon. Yes, even the very
word *gods* should go. The single word *God* alone should be
allowed to stand. He would close every temple in Egypt
except the temples to Aton.

The wildest excitement arose. Alack, the young Pharaoh
was mad! The people loved their old gods even while they
feared them. When Amon alone was taken, they still had
Hathor left, or Osiris and Isis and Horus and plenty of

Royal officers smash a statue of the cow-goddess, Hathor, to which the people cling. Akhnaton from the steps of the temple of Aton looks on sadly, while the weary soldiers returning from the wars wonder, in simple amazement, what it's all about, this smashing of the old gods and talking of a god of peace.

others besides.   They had not so much minded obeying the wishes of Pharaoh by singing praises to Aton, if afterward they could go and sacrifice to Ra, or to one of their ancient gods.   But to take away all their gods, to bring down upon them the vengeance of all those outraged powers!   The people were almost ready to rise up in revolt.   Confusion reigned in Egypt, men knew not what to think!

And soon, through the streets of the city, the weary messengers passing bore no more appeals for aid from generals in Asia.   Instead, they came announcing the fall of the last loyal cities, the death of the last loyal kings. And hot on the heels of these messengers, the broken and scattered garrisons came staggering back to Egypt, pursued to the very frontiers by victorious foreign hosts.   From the north, the Hittites poured into Syria. From the south the Khabiri swarmed over the land, while Aziru, the Amorite, snatched city after city.

Then the tribute so long paid to Egypt at last ceased altogether, and the government at home, weakened by what had occurred, could no more gather its taxes.

In the space of a few sad years, Egypt had been reduced from a great and rich world-power to a petty bankrupt state. Moreover Akhnaton saw now that though he had given up Syria in his deep and earnest desire to preach the gospel of peace, his people in Egypt did not understand the truth he had tried to teach them. It had not taken root in their hearts and would die when he was gone. It was not through him that the love of God was to be made known to the world.

Akhnaton's heart was broken; and when the last sorrowful news of the loss of his empire came, "the Beautiful Child of the Aton," "Lord of the Breath of Sweetness," a man now of thirty years, turned his face to the wall and died.

Thus ended the first great adventure in thinking. Akhnaton had seen the fact that there is one God only, a God who is wholly good and the source of life to the world. In an age aflame with war and greed he saw the first great vision of peace, of nations governed by love and mutual understanding instead of oppression and hate, and he failed, not because his vision was wrong, but because men's hearts were not yet ready to receive the truths he taught, and he had not sufficient wisdom to use the weapons of bronze when bronze was the only weapon before which Greed would bow, leaving the full understanding of all his glorious dreams to the slow, steady growth of time. Nevertheless, he left his vision to men, and to this day they are striving still to make his dreams come true.

Tut-ankh-amen hunting lions. This scene was painted on a casket found in his tomb. In the casket were treasured his baby glove, his infant hood and tippet, his jewelled buckles, and other childish keepsakes. Cairo Museum.

Tut-ankh-amen (Toot'onk-ah'men)
(1349-1343 B. C.)

Now unto Akhnaton and Nefertiti had been born in the days of their happiness seven daughters but no son.

Two at least of his little girls the King had called from their dolls to marry to little princes. These boys he had carefully trained in the beloved truths of the Aton, hoping they would keep his faith alive long after he was gone.

It was the elder of these boys who succeeded the King at his death, but the lad reigned only a year, leaving the throne to the second prince, a child some twelve years old. Tut-ankh-aton the boy was called, "Tut-having his-life-from-Aton," thus showing that from birth he had served Akhnaton's God.

But now the priests of Amon saw a boy on the throne, and they said: "We can work our will on such a little fellow!"

They surrounded young Tut (Toot) with servants who favored Amon. They threatened and overawed him.

For a time the boy held out, but he had no great urge

At the left, young Tut-ankh-amen sits at ease, in his splendid ceremonial head dress, while his wife, with delightful intimacy, adjusts his jewelled collar, approving his gorgeous apparel. Above is the sun-disk, symbol of Akhnaton's God, showing that the King is still faithful to Aton. (Chair back, Cairo Museum.) At the right, the young queen still wearing the side-lock of childhood, hands her husband bouquets of papyrus and lotus which maidens are gathering in the colored border below. (Ivory casket, Cairo Museum.)

within his soul, no strength of fire like Akhnaton. More-over, what had he seen? An empire that went to pieces under

A beautiful golden statuette of Tut-ankh-amen entering the Underworld on the back of a black leopard. (Cairo Museum.) At the left the King's feather fan and at the right a graceful, translucent, white alabaster vase.

Chiefs of Nubia and their families pay tribute to Tut-ankh-amen. These black people from the Upper Nile are now aping Egyptian magnificence. The chieftains' wives have splendid ear-rings, and ornaments; and one has a costly chariot and state umbrella, but she can find nothing better to pull her chariot than oxen. Below, the Negroes adore Pharaoh with extended arms, but the artist, with a humor which he would never have dared express before the days of Akhnaton, puts hands on the cows' horns to make them also adore Pharaoh. (Huy's Tomb, El Amarna.)

Akhnaton's rule, a people clamoring loudly to have their old gods back. After all, he was only a boy. In process of time he yielded,—Amon should be restored.

And when the priests had got the boy completely under their thumbs, they made him desert Akhnaton's city, and go

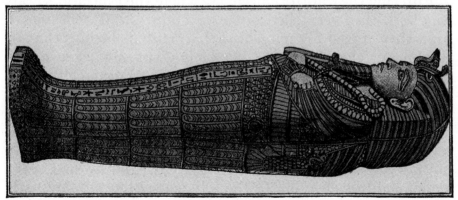

A miniature replica of Tut-ankh-amen's gold and inlaid coffin with a likeness of the Pharaoh. The word ankh is the name of the sign of life. (See page 204.) Therefore Tut-ankh-amen means Tut-with-life-from-Amon.

The goddess-guarded canopic chest of milk-white alabaster in the innermost recess of Tut-ankh-amen's tomb. In the chest are 4 receptacles whose stoppers are portrait busts of the king. In these receptacles, the king's heart, lungs, etc., were kept in small copies of his gold coffin as shown on page 223.

with them to Thebes; so the City-of-Dreams in the desert crumbled and fell into ruins.

Then they made the young Pharaoh change his name. No longer should he be called Tut-living-in-Aton. Henceforth let him be Tut-ankh-amen, that is Tut-living-in-Amon.

Thus came to an end completely Akhnaton's glorious dream.

The young King not only allowed the priests to hack out the name of Aton, and restore the name of Amon and the other gods of Egypt everywhere in the land, but he did not check the fury with which the priests of Amon now poured out the vials of their wrath on their dead foe, the hated Akhnaton. They called him a traitor, a heretic. They permitted no man to speak his name. On all official documents, they called him only "that criminal."

Entering the tomb of Queen Tiy where the Pharaoh's body was laid, they scratched out every figure that represented him, they erased his name from his coffin, believing that by this means they made the poor fellow an outcast, a nameless, hopeless wanderer in the shadowy World of Ghosts.

So Amon was restored as the greatest god of Egypt and the priesthood of Amon arose in greater power than before.

Then those who controlled the boy Pharaoh set themselves to regain the provinces lost in Asia, but Tut-ankh-amen's rule lasted no more than six years, for he died at the age of eighteen, leaving to the following Pharaoh, a sturdy veteran of ancient wars, Harm'hab by name, the problem

A glimpse of one of the rooms in the tomb of Tut-ankh-amen filled with confused heaps of treasures of art. This tomb was discovered by Howard Carter and the Earl of Carnarvon in 1922.

of really restoring to Egypt her ancient power and prestige.

In his short reign Tut-ankh-amen accomplished very little except to undo completely all the work of Akhnaton. He was one of the least among the Pharaohs, but his name became known throughout the world because of the discovery of his tomb in 1922.

This tomb was not so magnificent as many other Pharaoh's; it was only important because it was the first royal tomb discovered almost undisturbed by robbers.

Heaped in confusion about the rooms were furniture, chariots, vases; but nothing revealed more appealingly the youthfulness of the boy than one treasured little glove, kept by some loving care from the time when his hands were small, and the black side-lock of a child marked "The side-lock which his Majesty wore when he was a boy."

All the finely wrought treasures found in the young King's tomb reveal the exquisite workmanship of the artists of his time, emphasizing the fact that the art of Egypt reached its height in the days of the eighteenth dynasty, that marvelous line of great kings, who made and lost an empire.

Mummy of Ramses II and his head, drawn from the mummy. See Winifred K. Brunton: *Kings and Queens of Egypt.*

X
The Power of Egypt Declines
Ramses II, the Great
(1292-1225 B. C.)

After the days of Harmhab, there followed a line of fighting Pharaohs, Ram'ses I, Set'i I, and Ramses II, who once again made Egypt the mistress of an empire.

Ramses, the second, was the Grand Monarch of Egypt, conqueror and builder, living in great magnificence. He sat on his golden throne, a man of commanding presence, with high forehead and high arched nose like the beak of a great royal eagle.

Early in his boyhood, Ramses was trained in the ways of fighting and ruling; for his father, Seti I, made him his partner on the throne. And when Ramses himself became Pharaoh, he gathered together an army of 600,000 footmen, 24,000 horsemen, 27,000 chariots and 400 ships of war.

Marching north and south down the highways, his banners flying defiantly, he conquered chief after chief in Africa and Asia, always carving his name and his portrait on some outstanding rock; for Ramses the Great was a boaster, more proud and vainglorious than any of the other Pharaohs.

The chief enemies of Ramses were the Khe'ta or Hit'tites, the ancient foes of Akhnaton, who had seized much land in Syria that had once belonged to Egypt.

The Hittites were a powerful people, a race of many mixed tribes dwelling as hardy highlanders among the northwestern hills. Some were Mongolian, thin-faced and hungry-looking, having slanting eyes and high cheek-bones and wearing pigtails, or queues. Others resembled the Greeks with fine, straight, handsome features. Still others were Semitic Amorites with prominent hooked noses, low receding foreheads and heavily curled black beards.

The beautiful picture of Nefertari, the wife of Ramses II, led by Horus to the Underworld (from her tomb at Thebes).

Note her serpent ear-rings and her hands with the thumbs turned wrong side to. The Egyptians never learned to draw hands correctly and they always drew the face, the legs and feet turned completely to the side and the upper body turned straight to the front.

All these different people had been living in Asia Minor under their tribal chieftians since before 3000 B.C.

The Hittites used horses and chariots long before their neighbors, and in the mountains round about they had already found iron, a metal much harder than bronze, from which they were forging weapons to beat their enemies down, while iron in Egypt was still so rare that it was only used to adorn odd bits of jewelry and considered a precious metal, curious, costly and strange.

So precious was iron in Egypt that small bits of it were set in gold, just as if it were a valuable gem. This iron "Eye of Horus" was attached to a gold bangle and hung as an amulet on the breast of Tut-ankh-amen.

Awful Hittite gods; a Hittite warrior, and king with pigtails like the Chinese. See p. 216; Vol. II, pp. 50, 95, 104, 145.

The Kheta had not grown important, however, till about 1400 B. C., when Hat'tu-sil I began to extend his power by force of arms and alliances over other small Hittite kings, passing on to his son, the crafty Sub'bi-lu'li-u'ma, the leadership of a confederacy that gradually developed into a Hittite empire.

Sitting in his palace, guarded by grim rows of beasts in solemn rounded carvings, heavy and full of power, Subbi-luli-uma spun a web of intrigue. He wedded his daughter to one of the white-faced Aryan princes of the neighboring land of Mi-tan'ni; and when his enemy, Tush-rat'ta, the old King of Mitanni, died, he made his son-in-law the new king of the land, and so swallowed up Mitanni.

He incited the Amorite, Az'-i-ru, to his crafty dealings with Egypt in the days of Pharaoh Akhnaton; then he picked a quarrel with his dupe and put Aziru to a tribute.

So he made the Hittite Confederacy the greatest rival Egypt had in her ancient empire in Asia. For a hundred and fifty years his slant-eyed, grim faced descendants ruled vast stretches of land, little disturbed by Egypt, till the vigorous Seti I came pushing up to the northward. Seti was able, however, to make little headway against them; the real struggle remained for Ramses II, his son.

Now Me-tel'la, the Hittite emperor, knew he must conquer Egypt if he intended to keep his rich possessions in Syria. He gathered a mighty host and began advancing southward.

"Their number was endless," wrote a scribe. "Nothing like it has ever been seen! They covered the hills like grass-hoppers!"

But Ramses was not dismayed. He took the field in person, traversing the land of Canaan and pitching his camp near Kadesh which now belonged to the Kheta.

A busy place was that camp. Before the King's great pavilion, blacksmiths worked at their forges; soldiers squatted about, eating from savory bowls; men carried water in buckets from poles slung over their shoulders. Horses fed in the mangers. Footmen and charioteers chatted or fell to brawling, while some were chastised with whips.

The camp of Ramses II. The oblong structure on arches, is the wooden pavilion of the King. Five attendants kneel before his sleeping apartment which is watched over by two winged genii.

At the top of the picture a soldier mends a plough. Next him two soldiers squat over a cauldron of food while a man passes by with a pair of water buckets suspended at each end of a pole across his shoulders.

To the left horses feed in mangers, charioteers drag off chariots and a blacksmith before a brazier shoes a horse.

To the right infantry and charioteers arrive; and behind the king's pavilion an officer is about to be stabbed in a quarrel. Below, soldiers brawl and are punished; in the foreground to the right two Hittite spies are soundly beaten. (From the temple of Ramses II far south up the Nile at Abu Simbel.)

The royal chariot and great horses of Ramses are brought around from the stables. Four of the king's spearmen and two of his Sardinian body-guard with full moons on their helmets await the King's approach. These men from Sardinia amid the host of foreigners in the army of the king, show the presence in Egypt of the Sea-peoples, who later grew so powerful that Ramses III had to crush them. See page 236; also Vol. II, p. 150. (From Abu Simbel.)

Moreover many mixed races crowded this camp of Pharaoh's. No longer was the army composed solely of natives of Egypt. There were hosts of foreigners now, either hired or forced into service as members of conquered tribes. There were black Ethiopians, tattoed Libyans, picturesque Sardinians with full moons on their helmets, and handsome Bedouin tribesmen flourishing glistening spears.

At length two spies of the Kheta permitted the king's scouts to seize them and when they were dragged before Pharaoh, they falsely and craftily said: "The army of the Kheta, dreading the hosts of Egypt, has retreated forty leagues northward and lies beyond A-lep'po!"

Believing this story true and never suspecting the enemy near, Ramses set out next morning, attended only by his bodyguard, to go in search of the Hittites. The bulk of his powerful forces, the strong brigades of Amon, Ptah, and Ra, followed some distance behind him. But when two more spies were taken, Ramses became suspicious. Egyptian officers beat the spies and forced them to tell the truth. The army of the Kheta was almost upon the Egyptians!

Hastily calling a council of war, Ramses sent off messengers to bid the brigade of Amon hurry up to join him, but at this critical moment, the Kheta emerged from their ambush and threw themselves between Pharaoh and all the rest of his host.

Thus surrounded and cut off from the three brigades in the rear, Ramses, with desperate valor, flung himself into the combat. Bending his great war bow, he stood erect in his chariot which was drawn by his two faithful steeds, "Nura" and "Victory to Thebes." So great were his deeds that day, that they were afterward sung in the famous *Poem of Pentaur*.

Then the king stood forth, and, radiant with courage,
He looked like the sun-god, armed and eager for battle.
The noble steeds that bore him,—
"Victory to Thebes" was the name of one;
The other one was called "Nura,"
Colts they were, bred in his stables.
Up sprang the King and threw himself on the foe,
On the swaying ranks of the worthless Kheta.
He stood alone—alone, and no man with him!

Ramses standing entirely alone charges the Hittites in the battle of Kadesh. Beneath his chariot is the river Orontes into which his enemy hurl themselves. Below three powerful warriors ride in each Hittite chariot. (A relief from the Ramesseum, Thebes.) Ramses ordered the Poem of Pentaur carved on the walls of five temples.

As thus the King stood forth, all eyes were on him,
And soon he was swallowed up by the mass of men and horses,
And by the enemy's chariots, ten thousand five hundred in
    number.
Dense the array of the worthless Kheta;
Each chariot carried three warriors,
All foes to the King, and bound to each other like brothers.

"Not a prince is with me, not a captain,
Not an archer, none to guide my horses!
Fled the riders! Fled my troops and horsemen—
By my side not one is now left standing!"
Thus spake the King and raised his voice in prayer:
"Great father Amon, I have known thee well,
And can the father thus forget his son?
I call on thee. But save me and thy glory
Shall fill the world from East to West!"

Yea, so his cry rang forth,
And Amon came himself appearing at his call,
And gave his hand to Pharaoh, shouting loud in triumph:
"Thine help is here at hand, O Ramses! I uphold thee!"

Then with his right hand, Pharaoh scattered arrows,
And with his left he swung his deadly weapon—
Felling those, his foes—
None found a hand to fight; they could not shoot;
Nor dared they hurl the spear, but at his coming, fled
Headlong into the river!

The Kheta flee through the river. The King of Aleppo has swallowed so much water that his soldiers hold him upside down to empty him. This picture completes the one on page 231.

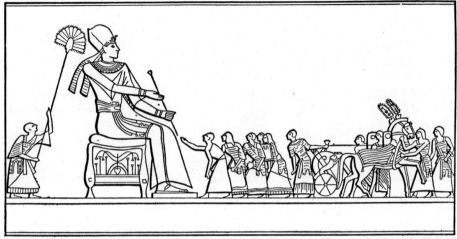

Ramses enthroned, receives the congratulations of his officers after the victory. (From the temple at Abu Simbel.)

Then there came, fighting their way from the rear, the brigades of Amon, Ra and Ptah, which completed the rout of the Kheta.

All the hosts of Egypt returned in triumph to camp, bringing with them the enemy's cattle and long lines of wretched prisoners, while scribes counted hands of the slain before the chariot of Ramses.

The next day at sunrise came the Prince of the Kheta himself to make his peace with Pharaoh.

Then Ramses went back to Egypt, but when the Hittites found their great and powerful enemy safely out of their way, they refused to bow the neck in real submission to him.

For fifteen years they resisted, and that with such force and success that Ramses was glad at last to make a treaty with Hat'-tu-sil II by taking his daughter to wife. This treaty was solemnly engraved upon a tablet of silver and in it the Hittite ruler was no longer called "Vile Chief" but "Great King," the title of Pharaoh himself. So ended the long struggle between Ramses and the Hittites.

Now all the vast conquests of Ramses brought such

The Great Hall built by Ramses II at Kar'nak. In this wonderful suburb of Thebes were built the most beautiful temples ever erected in Egypt. Many Pharaohs enriched this spot with colossal statues, colorful buildings, obelisks, and impressive avenues of sphinxes that led up from the river. See pages 171 and 189.

wealth to his treasury that he was able to build the greatest number of splendid structures ever erected by a single king in Egypt. Palaces, temples, storehouses, the great Hall of Columns at Karnak he built, and in addition to these, he wrote his name on many another structure erected by some former Pharaoh, erasing the name of his predecessor and leaving only his own.

Nor did the great Pharaoh care how painfully workmen toiled, or even died in his service, building those mighty structures. It was doubtless in work on his cities that the suffering tribes of Israel endured such painful affliction beneath their cruel taskmasters, driven by lash of whips to endless toil in the burning heat and the glaring sunshine of Egypt.

Ramses cared not at all for the wailing of the oppressed; his heart knew little pity for the humble among his subjects. To build, to conquer, to hold, were all the desires he knew; and for sixty-seven years he continued to rule in Egypt. At last he sat on the throne, an old man, nearing his hundredth year, with fifty-nine dutiful daughters and a hundred and eleven sons to magnify his pride and proclaim him with proper praises the greatest of all the Pharaohs.

Four figures of Ramses III from the tomb of his son at Thebes. They show the different garments worn in different seasons of the year. To the left is the thin transparent linen kilt of summer. Next, in spring and fall the King adds an overkilt, or he covers the upper part of his body with thin linen as in the third figure. Lastly, in winter he wears a thick kilt and thick colored bands to form a waist with sleeves. To the right is a lady of this period. (Cairo Museum.) Note how elaborate wigs and garments have grown and compare with the simplicity of the Old Kingdom.

A Weakened Egypt

After the death of Ramses the Great and Mer-ne'ptah, his son, there came only one more vigorous reign before Egypt fell back again into days of disorder and weakness.

Figures of Egypt's conquered enemies in the days of Ramses III. Colored enamel plaques from his temple at Medinet Habu. (1.) Syrian. (2.) Libyan. (3.) Hittite. (4.) Sicilian. (Cairo Museum.) (5.) Philistine. (6.) Ethiopian. (Boston Museum.) For the battle of Ramses III with the Sea Peoples, see Vol. II, p. 150.

The high priest of Amon decorated by Ramses IX. So important has become the office of High Priest that the priest's figure is made as large as that of the king, whereas in older pictures the king was always drawn many times larger than all other figures.

This was the reign of Ramses III, who sailed forth with his warships and drove from the shores of Egypt the plundering galleys of the Sea-Peoples, pirates from Cyprus, Crete, and other Aegean Isles, who had left their homes and fled before the terrific onslaughts of hordes of Greek barbarians, wild, uncivilized Dorians from the mountains of North-central Greece.

Nine more kings, each bearing the name of Ramses, followed this Ramses III, and ruled Egypt with ever-weakening power for about a hundred years. Then at last the High Priest of Amon, Her'hor by name, became the real ruler while the weak King, Ramses XII, sat on the throne of the Pharaohs, a ruler only in name, and a second king, Nes-u-ba-neb'ded, maintained himself in the Delta.

Nothing shows better the confusion of the Empire in those days and the loss of Egypt's power and prestige in Syria, than the true tale of the wanderings of that poor old fellow Wen'a-mon who was sent by Herhor to Syria.

Gone were the good old days when an envoy of Egypt had only to lift his finger to send the Princelings of Syria running to do his bidding. The Princes of Syria now, half contemptuous of their old mistress, paid only most grudging attention to any demands of Egypt.

Wenamon set out from Thebes with no ships and no attendants, dependent on such courtesy as he might meet on the way, and having in place of Pharaoh's army, only a little stone figure, the image of Amon, the god, with which to impress the Syrians and make them heed his requests.

The Misfortunes of Wenamon*
(1113 B. C.)

In Upper Egypt, Herhor, High Priest of Amon, ruled. In Lower Egypt, Nes'u-ba-neb'ded, Prince of Tanis, ruled.

Now Herhor undertook to build a barge-of-ceremony to bear upon the Nile the image of his god. Therefore he sent for me, Wen'a-mon, eldest of the Hall of the Temple, to bid me fetch cedar wood.

"Proceed to the Prince of Byblos," he said, "and procure me cedar from Lebanon to make a state barge for our god."

Then he gave me letters to princes of Syria, with such money as he could spare, entrusting to me likewise a little image of Amon, to let it be known in Syria that, though my treasure was small, I came on the business of Amon.

On the sixteenth day of the eleventh month of the fifth year of the reign of Ramses XII, I set out by boat for Tanis where I delivered to Nes'u-ba-neb'ded my letters of introduction. Then Nesubanebded sent me to sea in a ship with a Syrian skipper, a sorry sort of vessel, but the best he could afford.

Scarcely had we left port, when I found I had left behind in the hands of Nesubanebded my letters of introduction. Therefore I said to the skipper:

"A great misfortune has befallen me. I have left my letters behind. I pray you turn back, that I may recover my loss."

But the skipper paid no heed. He kept the nose of his vessel ever heading for Syria, nor would he obey my bidding. Then my heart was heavy within me and I cried in my distress: "How shall I be received in Syria with naught in writing to show that I come on business of state?"

Nevertheless, we proceeded. We sailed past Ashdod and Askelon, and at last put into port to replenish supplies at Dor, a city of Sicilians at the foot of the ridge of Mt. Carmel.

*This story is described in a *History of Egypt* by J. M. Breasted and *The Glory of the Pharaohs* by Arthur Weigall. In it Ramses XII is mentioned only once and that to date the tale. It is Her'hor and Nes'u-ba-neb'ded whom Wenamon looks upon as the real rulers of Egypt.

Egyptian-Syrian commerce in the days of Wenamon. Note the Syrians in their long woolen robes of twisted strips standing on the deck with Egyptian sailors, and other Syrians on shore. (From a New Kingdom tomb at Thebes.)

Hearing that an envoy of the High Priest of Amon-ra was arrived in the harbor of Dor, King Bed'el sent me a gift, a joint of beef, some loaves of bread and a jar of wine.

But even as I feasted, a second misfortune befell me. A wretched sailor of Dor, secretly entered my cabin and found the hiding place where I kept the gold and silver entrusted to me by Herhor. He stole the treasure and left the ship, losing himself from sight mid the maze of narrow streets in this miserable city of Dor.

I entered my cabin; I found my loss; I sat down distracted with grief. I wailed; I mourned; I listed my stolen treasure.

One jar containing gold amounting to........ 5 debens
Four jars containing silver amounting to....20 debens
*One wallet containing silver amounting to....11 debens**

No letters of introduction and no money to buy the wood!

Early the following morning I hastened off to King Bedel.

*A sorry total of $14,000—a paltry sum with which to purchase the costly cedar wood.

"I have been robbed in your harbor!" I cried. "And since you are King of this land, you are responsible for this crime. You must return my money which belongs to Nesubanebded and Herhor, my lord, and the other nobles of Egypt."

But the King of Dor made answer:

"With all due respect to your Excellency, I know nothing of this matter. If the thief had been one of my subjects, I would advance you the sum while my servants searched for the thief. But the villain must be from your own ship. Who else would know where the treasure was hid? Tarry for a few days and I will seek the fellow!"

For nine days I waited, hoping; but when the tenth day dawned, I went to the palace again.

"Look you!" I cried to the King. "You have not found my money! Therefore, pay me yourself!"

But the King cried roughly: "Be silent!"

So I took myself off in anger, and sailed out to sea again.

In time we put in at Tyre and there I saw on the wharf a party of wretched Sicilians, traveling on business from Dor. So I ordered my men to fall on them, and while they strug-

Wenamon stands by while his men overpower the Sicilians. Costume of Sicilians from figure 4, page 235.

gled together, I snatched a bag of silver away from the wretched fellows; and I said:

"I will keep your money until you find mine for me! Was it not a Sicilian from Dor who stole away my treasures?"

And I hurried aboard my ship and sailed with my men to Byblos. But as we drew near the city, my heart was heavy within me, for I had no letters and I knew not whether those wretched Sicilians had made complaint concerning me.

News of my ship's arrival was brought to the King of Byblos, but he sent his Harbor Master to say:

"Get you out of this harbor!"

And every day for 29 days, the Harbor Master repeated: "Get you out of this harbor!"

Then I caused it to be noised abroad that I had with me a sacred image of Amon, the giver of life and health, and that evil would fall on the city who turned this god away.

And Zak'ar Ba'al, Prince of Byblos, was offering sacrifice to his god, when a noble youth in his train was seized with prophetic frenzy and in divine ecstasy cried:

"Summon this envoy of Amon who bears the image of his god. Treat him well and dismiss him with honor!"

So the Prince of Byblos, moved by this word, sent his Harbor Master to fetch me. And the Harbor Master found me, discouraged by my long waiting, walking in the darkness along the deserted quay, about to embark for Egypt and bearing in my arms the sacred image of Amon.

On the following morning he led me before the Prince in the fortress upon the seashore. I found the Prince sitting in his upper chamber, leaning his back against a window, while the waves of the Syrian Sea beat on the shore below.

Then the Prince of Byblos said:

"If you are truly an envoy come unto me from Herhor, High Priest of the great Amon-ra, where is the letter from Herhor which should be in your hand?"

"I gave my letters to Nesubanebded," I replied.

Then the Prince of Byblos was wroth and he said:

"Look you! If you came in truth from Nesubanebded, why have you such a sorry ship and such a sorry crew? Why have you no letters, no retinue, and so paltry a sum of silver?"

"Nesubanebded had at the time no better ship to give me," I hasted to reply, but the Prince of Byblos answered:

"There are twenty better ships in my harbor at this very moment, all come from Nesubanebded, and at Sidon lie 10,000 better ships all of them come from Egypt."

Then I was silent in that great hour. And the King of Byblos said: "On what business have you come hither?"

I said to him, "I have come after timber to build the great and august barge of Amon-ra, King of the Gods. Your fathers furnished wood for this purpose and you will do it likewise."

He said to me, "My fathers indeed furnished timber but they were paid for so doing. Pharaoh sent them in payment six vessels of produce of Egypt."

And he caused one to bring his father's account book before him; and he read in my presence the amount which that Pharaoh had paid to his sire. And he said:

"My fathers paid no tribute to Egypt. I am neither your servant nor the servant of Amon. If I cry out to the Lebanon, the heavens open and the logs lie here on the shores of the sea. But this I will not do without the proper payment! Once art and fine craftsmanship came out from Egypt and teaching came forth from the Nile-land to reach my home here in Byblos. How does it come about that a land, once so great as Egypt, has sent an envoy like you to make the journey hither in such a miserable fashion?"

"O guilty one," I cried, "there is no ship on the Nile which Amon does not own! His is the sea and his this Lebanon, of which you say, 'It is mine!' For twenty nine days you have

kept this great god waiting! Now as for Amon-ra, he is lord
of life and health and he was the lord of thy fathers to whom
they sacrificed. If you do the bidding of Amon, you shall
prosper and be in health. Let me send my scribe to Nesubanebded, that he may send me treasure to pay you for the
timber. Moreover, when I return to Egypt, I will send you
any trifle that may still be owing to you."

So I sent unto Nesubanebded and in forty-eight days' time
my messenger returned bringing 5 golden vases; 5 silver
vases; 20 garments of linen; 500 rolls of papyrus; 5 measures
of dried fish; 20 measures of lentils; 500 ox-hides, and 500
coils of rope. Moreover, in the name of Amon-ra, I promised
to the Prince of Byblos, over and above all this, 10,000 years
more of heavenly life than that granted other mortals!

With this present the Prince was content. He sent three
hundred men with three hundred oxen and overseers to fell
the cedar trees. And eight months after the day when I first
set sail from Tanis, I walked on the shores of Byblos beneath
the state umbrella of Zakar Baal, the Prince, and he pointed
out to me all the cedar logs, lying ready upon the shore.

But when I stood alone, rejoicing in this success, I lifted mine eyes to seaward and beheld eleven ships sailing toward me swiftly. Presently one on shore cried out: "What is your business here?"

"We are men of Dor," shouted the newcomers, "come to arrest one Wenamon. Let no ship of his escape!"

On hearing this dreadful news, I flung myself on the sand! I cast dust on my head! I burst out into weeping!

Now the Chief Scribe sat in the window and when he saw me lament he came and said: "What aileth you?"

"Surely you see these birds which descend on Egypt?" I groaned. "You see who cometh to seize me?"

Then the Chief Scribe told the Prince, and the Prince looked out of the window and saw the Sicilian ships anchored as a barrier across the mouth of the harbor. And he saw me on the shore, casting sand on my head. And his heart was moved to pity and he sent me two jars of wine and a roast of mutton to cheer me. But I only wept the more. Then he sent me a dancing girl to amuse me and lift up my spirit. But all was of no avail. I looked on the ships and I wept.

The following morning came men from the ships to tell the Prince of Byblos that they sought for the envoy Wenamon who had robbed one of their countrymen of 31 debens of silver. But the Prince replied to them:

"I cannot arrest an envoy of Amon within my territory. I will only send him away and you shall pursue and arrest him!"

The Sicilians approved the plan. They delighted to think of pursuing me as the lion pursueth his prey, as the hunter pursueth his quarry. And so they drew off from the city to lie in wait for me, when my ship should sail out of the harbor.

Great was my grief and my fear. I entered my ship and set sail. Trembling, I watched the vessel glide on its way from the harbor, awaiting the awful moment when the huntsmen lying in wait, should come and pounce down upon me.

But when we sailed into the open sea, a terrible storm was brewing. There sprang up a sudden wind that threatened death and destruction.

And now I dared not go back, for behind me lay the Sicilians. I must needs continue my course out into the sea and the tempest. Mine enemies came not after me. They durst not put forth in the storm.

The tempest drove me far out of my course and cast me up at last on the coast of the island of Cyprus.

Chariots and horsemen such as Wenamon saw on the island of Cyprus, whither he was carried by the storm. From an ancient sarcophagus found in Cyprus and now in the Metropolitan Museum, New York. This island, lying fairly near Syria, yet racially connected with Crete and the Mediterranean peoples, was an interesting mixture of Cretan, Assyrian and Egyptian civilizations.

Such people as Wenamon saw in Cyprus. The man to the left wears a peculiar native Cyp'ri-ote costume, a skin-tight upper tunic, and drawers like a bathing suit, or an acrobat's trunks. Across his forehead is a broad frontlet. The lady stepping forward so briskly, her head held high, her right hand raised in a gesture of command, her left hand holding up her skirt, shows what Queen Hat'i-ba must have been like. Her garments resemble those of Assyria, a long tunic with a cloak over it, necklaces, pendant ear-rings, lion-headed bracelets, and a rectangular satchel slung by a belt from the left shoulder. The princely gentleman at the right, is in a Cypriote variety of the Egyptian costume, only that his kilt, instead of being plain, is richly embroidered with an eye, a Medusa head with coiled snakes and Egyptian winged ureaus snakes. From the Cesnola Collection, Metropolitan Museum, New York.

And when I went ashore from the wreck of my battered ship accompanied by the crew, the populace of the island fell upon me to kill me. They dragged me to the palace of Hat'i-ba the Queen; but as I neared the building, the Queen herself came out, surrounded by her attendants.

Then I flung myself at her feet crying:

"Surely some one here can speak the language of Egypt!"

And one of the Queen's attendants answered me in Egyptian; whereon, this man translating, I said unto the Queen:

"I have heard as far as Thebes, that though there be injustice in every other land, yet justice is found in Cyprus! How then have I met with such injustice here?"

The Queen replied: "Indeed! What is this that thou sayest to me?"

I answered her: "If the sea raged and the wind drove me

Wenamon pleads for his life before the Queen of Cyprus. Figure of the Queen is taken from the little statuette page 245. The man who translates her words into Egyptian for Wenamon, wears the Egypto-Cypriote costume, page 245. Some of her other attendants wear Assyrio-Cypriote robes. The men who hold Wenamon's followers, wear the native costume like an acrobat's trunk, developed from the loin-cloth of Crete. (See page 245). The beautiful vase with grazing horses, long-legged birds and geometric designs was found in Cyprus and is now in the Metropolitan Museum, New York. See reference to Nesubenebded under picture, Vol II, p. 54.

hither, why should you let your people take advantage of me to slay me? I am a messenger of Amon-ra, King of the Gods, for whom Egypt will seek unceasingly. As for my crew, they are men of Byblos. If you kill them, their lord will find ten such crews belonging to you and slay them all in punishment."

With this the Queen was impressed. She ordered the mob to set me free and she said unto me:

"You and your crew shall pass the night here in safety."*

From Cyprus poor old Wenamon found his way home again; trembling, groaning and weak in the age of Egypt's weakness,—how different from young Harkhuf and his bold adventurous journeys in the days of Egypt's young strength!

*Here this manuscript ends. The rest was destroyed by peasants, who found the original papyrus and used it to light a fire, not guessing its value. However, Wenamon certainly returned in safety since he lived to write this tale.

The Last Days of Egypt

The line of Priest-Kings which followed Herhor, made Thebes independent and often governed all Egypt, but being weak themselves, they hired wild Libyan troops, barbarians from the desert, to fight their battles for them. Thus in 945 B.C., She'shonk, a Libyan chief, overthrew the last Priest-King and made himself the Pharaoh. For two hundred years his descendants ruled a turbulent land till a black King of Na-pa'ta far away up the Nile, one Pi-ankh'i by name, came down and forced the Egyptians to acknowledge him as their King. Thus the once proud Egypt first bowed the neck to desert-dwellers and then to a glistening black Negro. But a worse fate still was in store. There was now rising up in Asia, a powerful fighting nation, Assyria, the pillager, determined to make herself the war-lord of the world. Two Kings of Assyria, Es'ar-had'don and As'sur-ba'ni-pal, came down in succession, drove the black men back to Ethiopia and possessed themselves of Egypt. Only one native Egyptian, Psam'tik, King of Sa'is, a district in the Delta, continued the struggle against them. Hiring Greek mercenaries, Psamtik drove out the Assyrians and united all Egypt under him in 663 B.C. Luckily, too, for him, Assyria's powerful neighbors, now rising up against her, kept her busy at home. Psamtik thus found himself free to build Egypt up again, to restore one last moment of glory to the slowly dying nation.

Es'ar-had'don, great King of Assyria and conqueror of Egypt, holds the tiny kneeling figure of Tahar'ka, the black Pharaoh of Egypt, ringed through the nose. In Egypt, Taharka had proudly ordered his portrait carved with classic Egyptian features, but the great Assyrian King, flinging scorn in his captive's face, showed him as he really was, an unfortunate little Negro, crouching at the Great King's feet and led about by a leading-string ringed through his broad flat nose. See Vol. II, p. 77. For Pharaoh Ne'cho see Vol. II, p. 239; for Neb-u-chad-nez'zar Vol. II, p. 82; Ho'phra Vol. II, pp. 249-251, 259.

Under this able and vigorous King, there came a rebirth of energy, a revival of life and activity in industry, commerce and art. Fondly dwelling on the good old days, Egypt lifted her head and under these Kings of Sais, for nearly a hundred years she rivaled her glorious youth. But when Ne'cho succeeded Psamtik, he began to dream of once again regaining Egypt's lost empire in Asia. Advancing to the Euphrates, he carried things with a high hand while Assyria was tottering; but when Assyria fell before the Babylonians and a new Babylonian war-lord, the mighty Neb-u-chad-nez'zar, came down into Syria, Necho was sorely defeated. His grandson, Pharaoh Ho'phra, accomplished no more when he tried to stir the smaller nations up to revolt against Nebuchadnezzar. After that Egypt made no further attempts to win an empire in Asia. Henceforth she stayed at home.

In 525 B.C. the Persians conquered Egypt and never, save for some short interval, did a native rule Egypt again. Alexander of Macedon, the conquering hero of the Greeks, took the land from the Persians and the Greek line of the Ptolemies ruled for three hundred years. Thus Egypt fell at last from the place which she had held for some three thousand years as foremost nation of the ancient world.

It was in Egypt that people first grew out of the Stone Age, and real history, written down on stone and papyrus, began. It was here that men discovered how to irrigate their farm-lands, invented writing, the calendar and the shadow clock. Egyptians were the first adventurers and explorers, penetrating into far-off lands and trading with other peoples. They were the first great builders, erecting monumental structures of enduring grandeur and strength. They were the first great architects, artists, sculptors, and craftsmen. They were the first great nation to work out a system of government and to unite many races into a far-reaching empire under the rule of one King.

SUMMARY OF VOLUME ONE

OUR STORY begins around 150,000 years ago, describing the kind of life led in the Old Stone Age by such a man as the one shown on page 12, whose skull was found at Piltdown in England. In these earliest days man knew practically nothing—he could talk only by making a few crude sounds, he had no home, no clothing, no weapons except a club and a stone. He was occupied solely in meeting his material needs and those of his family, in getting food for them to eat and protecting them from savage enemies. It is from this zero point that we trace his rise in civilization. Having as yet so few words, he could not exchange ideas with other men, and he roamed about only with his own family. So he progressed very slowly, since culture grows by the exchange and accumulation of ideas. Though this Old Stone Age lasted for at least 100,000 years, man learned only four things during all that time. He learned to protect himself against cold by wearing the fur of animals, to live in a shelter or cave, to chip stone into crude fist hatchets and to make fire to keep himself warm.

Then came the Middle Stone Age, the age of improved stone tools, when the bow and arrow were invented and men no longer had to fight with beasts at close range but could substitute skill for brute strength. This period lasted about 20,000 years instead of 100,000. Building on what had gone before, man could now progress less slowly. Having discovered how to meet his primal needs for food, clothing, shelter and protection, he could begin to find means to express himself—to express himself in language, in dancing, and in drawing pictures. In a painting from this period, reproduced on page 29, fighting bowmen are shown in such vigorous, spirited action that one can actually feel the strain and heat of a real fight, though nothing is used in the picture but lines and dots.

After the Middle Stone Age came the Late Stone Age, or the age of polished stone, which lasted only about 7,000 years in contrast to the 20,000 of the preceding period, again proving how much faster men can progress when the ball of accumulating knowledge really gets rolling. In this Late Stone Age men learned how to weave cloth and make simple pots out of clay and they developed a love for beauty, fashioning shells into jewelry and decorating their pottery by painting it with colored designs. Instead of living in caves they lived in houses of wattles or logs, they learned to domesticate animals and plants and how to farm, so they did not always have to hunt to get food. Then since they were no longer obliged to roam about seeking animals to kill, they began to live together in little villages, instead of wandering alone with their families as they had for thousands of years. And as these villages slowly grew into towns certain men stopped farming because they were better fitted to work at making things—tables and chairs, perhaps—and they exchanged what they made for the produce raised on the farms, thus starting the system of barter, which was the beginning of business and trade.

But no sooner had they begun to live together than questions of relationship arose. Men had to choose a leader or chief and begin to consider problems of government that mutual rights might be respected and common work carried on. So in the three periods of the Stone Age we find the whole problem of man presented—first, his necessity to meet his most pressing material needs; second, his innate desire for expression in ever richer fullness; third, the question of relationships and government in a constantly developing social order.

TOWARD THE END of the Late Stone Age at least one country, Egypt, had attained a high degree of culture. It was in Egypt that men worked out the first sign pictures as a primitive form of writing and began to record their history, not only in carvings on stone, but on a kind of paper, made of papyrus reeds. It was there, too, that their minds reached out to explain the causes of all the strange and wonderful phenomena of life, so stories of the gods arose and religion had its beginnings. Then finally about 4000 B.C., Egyptian explorers found copper in the Sinai Desert, and this discovery ended that long period of more than 150,000 years when men had had only stone weapons and tools, starting them off into the present age of metal.

From this point we go on to a definite history of Egypt, beginning with the Old Kingdom, the period of the great pyramid builders. Founded by Pharaoh Menes, who united the two lands of the Nile, Upper and Lower Egypt, into one kingdom before 3400 B.C., the Old Kingdom was one of the finest eras in all Egyptian history. It was an age of simplicity, quiet elegance, dignity, youthful freshness and strength. Egyptian sculptors now began to make lifelike portrait statues of men and women and a beautiful architecture arose. Houses and public buildings were adorned with pillars capped at the top with capitals in the form of a lotus bud, a papyrus flower or a circle of palm leaves, and the interiors of these buildings were decorated with splendidly painted frescoes, showing nobles hunting, merchants bartering, and other peaceful scenes of pleasant everyday life.

But most impressive of all the monuments left from this Old Kingdom are the three pyramids at Gizeh and the huge figure of the Sphynx, which rise from the sands of the desert inexpressibly grand.

The builder of the largest of these pyramids was King Khufu, sometimes called King Cheops, and some years ago the tomb of his mother, Queen Hetep-heres, was discovered. It contained her delicate gold-inlaid carrying chair and her traveling pavilion or tent, with its graceful little posts of gold. Today these things are in the museum at Cairo and on my visit to Egypt I pored over them for hours. There were her chair, her bed and camp stool, her tent, her anklets and many of her other dainty and beautiful personal belongings, all making this fine lady and the manner of life she had led in the distant age of the pyramid-builders seem as alive and real to my fancy as the life of the present about me.

The Old Kingdom also produced the first great explorers, and since I have tried, wherever I could, to include something, either from the literature of a country or from its actual records, I have chosen the true, but little-known story of the explorer, Harkhuf, to illustrate the adventurous spirit of the strong young Egypt of this period.

Harkhuf went up the Nile into the country of the fierce black Negro tribes, facing dangers every step of the way. He went also into the land of the Libyans, those savage, barbaric white warriors, who tattooed their bodies and roved through the Libyan Desert in hostile, threatening bands. Constantly he pushed forward the boundaries of human knowledge, enlarging the size of Egypt's hitherto little world. And the story of the boy king, Pepi, for whom he got a dancing pigmy, is full of human interest. Having been informed that Harkhuf was about to set out down the Nile, bringing the pigmy to him, the eager little boy, who was only six years old, had a letter written to the great explorer. First referring to himself grandiloquently as My Majesty, King of Upper and Lower Egypt, he burst forth with all the childish eagerness of any little boy about to receive a new toy. Demanding that the pigmy should be brought to him at once, he ordered Harkhuf to appoint trustworthy men to watch the dwarf all day on the boat, so he should not fall into the water, and others to sleep beside him and look at him ten times every night to make sure that he was safe.

This letter from little Pepi Harkhuf treasured so greatly that he had it carved on his tomb. The tomb is across from Aswan at the First Cataract of the Nile and is little visited, but I took a guide and crawled up to its doorway, photographing some of the pictures and hieroglyphs whereby Harkhuf immortalized this story.

The Old Kingdom ended in disorders when the nobles, growing ever more rich and powerful, threw off the rule of their Pharaohs, appearing as the first group of men in history to demand an extension of power beyond that of a king or a chief. But having no unity among themselves and being jealous of each other, these nobles created only strife and confusion, so trade, exploration, and all the other glorious activities of the vigorous Old Kingdom, ceased. Slowly the boundaries of Egypt shrank before inroads from Negro tribes and from the wandering men of the desert while all the land suffered from famine, robbery, violence, and distress.

IT WAS AMENEMHET I, the first Pharaoh of the famous Twelfth Dynasty, who around 2000 B. C. finally gave the land peace and founded the Middle Kingdom, though he could not entirely suppress the nobles or make them over into mere servants of the king, as they had been in earlier days. But he did unite them into a league, owing allegiance to Pharaoh, with the payment of taxes to him and service in time of war. Thus he prepared the way for Egypt to enter upon an age of even greater prosperity than that of the fine Old Kingdom. Once more Egyptians grew adventurous in commerce, trade and explorations. Not only did they go up the Nile and across to the island of Crete but they began also to make frequent journeys to Asia, especially to Syria and Canaan, which was later to be Palestine. Again Egypt's world was enlarging.

To illustrate this period of increasing contact with Asia I have chosen the story the soldier and courtier, Sinuhe, told of his own adventures in Syria. A good friend of Amenemhet and his Queen, Sinuhe was out in the desert with the army under Prince Sesostris, the heir to the throne, when Amenemhet died and Sinuhe overheard conspirators plotting to make another son of Amenemhet ruler before Sesostris could return to the capital city, Thebes. So Sinuhe, innocent though he was, fell into a panic lest he should be suspected of having a part in the plot. Fleeing from the camp in terror, he made his way, with many adventures, all the long distance north into Canaan and Syria at just about the same time when the patriarch, Abraham, was also journeying into that land. There he met wandering chieftains, following their flocks and herds and living as Abraham did in tents. Afraid to go back to Egypt, he lingered for years in Syria, wedding the daughter of a prince, becoming himself the chief of a tribe, and living, like the Syrians, in a tent, with flocks and herds of his own. He had grown old among the Syrians, always yearning in his heart for Egypt, when Sesostris, who had long been Pharaoh, heard what had happened to him and summoned him home. So Sinuhe at last returned with joy to his native land.

The story of Sinuhe is true but during this adventurous period, the imagination of men started soaring on the wings of fancy and fairy tales began. So beside true stories, like that of Sinuhe, we have from this period "The Story of the Shipwrecked Sailor" (page 155) wherein a shipwrecked mariner meets a mysterious bearded serpent who magically aids him to return in safety to his home. In all ways this Middle Kingdom was a period of great imaginative expansion. Art and architecture flourished, materials for clothing, no longer white as they had been in the Old Kingdom, were gaily colored and figured, wigs became more elaborate, armlets, anklets, and all kinds of jewelry more in demand.

THEN THE LIGHT in Egypt went out again, for a horde of Asiatic barbarians, led by the Hyksos, or Shepherd Kings, came down and plundered the land, destroying the Middle Kingdom and ruling Egypt for a hundred years. Not until 1600 B. C. did Pharaoh Ahmose succeed in driving out these Shepherd Kings, thereby founding the powerful Eighteenth Dynasty, the family who changed Egypt from a simple kingdom into a mighty empire ruling other lands.

Thutmose I, the first great conqueror of this line, set out to extend the rule of Egypt into Asia, and with that, the whole spirit of his people changed. No longer did they paint peaceful scenes of nobles hunting in boats among the papyrus reeds or merchants calmly bartering. Now they showed in their frescoes, processions of captive nations—Asiatics, Negroes, Libyans, tied with lotus and papyrus stems to indicate that they were bound beneath the yoke of Egypt. Egypt had at last become a military nation and its youth was all aflame with glamorous dreams of war and conquest. Everywhere the land resounded with the singing of hymns of victory while even the folk tales the people told, like "The Prince and the Three Dooms," (page 195) reflected the spirit of war and ever expanding empire.

When such a state as this appears in any nation it is an indubitable sign of the beginning of the end. Again and again has the same thing happened. A nation begins in simplicity with all the sturdy virtues, its abilities increase, it rises to a climax of attainment in every line, then it starts to feel its own power and the urge to exercise it over weaker nations. And as it conquers more and more territory, it grows in wealth, finally attaining so much luxury and ease that it starts to decline, to grow lazy and weak, until at last it is swallowed up by some fresher, more vigorous power.

However, one of this powerful Eighteenth Dynasty held back the stream of war and conquest for a time and this one person was a woman. Fifteen hundred years before Christ, Queen Hatshepsut, the first great woman appeared in history. She was the eldest daughter of Thutmose I, a vigorous, capable girl, whom her father regarded as the ablest of all his children and named as his successor. But on the death of her father, the people, accustomed from the time of the Stone Age to regard all authority as vested in the physically stronger sex, men, refused to accept a woman as their ruler. Her struggles against this prejudice were long and dramatic. And she was finally able to solve it only by insisting on being addressed as King, not Queen, and by appearing often in men's clothes with her chin adorned by the false beard, enclosed in a fine enameled case, which only Pharaohs had the right to wear. Moreover, still perplexed by the question of how to do what had been considered a man's job while she still remained a woman, Hatshepsut, in various pronouncements, mixed up *he's* and *she's* in a most remarkable way. Having erected a great stone pillar in honor of her father she had carved on it this inscription—"*His* Majesty gave these obelisks to *her* father."

But Hatshepsut proved to be a splendid ruler, who devoted her energies to building and organizing, not to war. In many ways her reign was like that of another great queen, Elizabeth of England, for she encouraged the arts and sent out many explorers into foreign countries.

Then in time Hatshepsut died and her nephew, Thutmose III, bursting with pent up energies and all those warlike propensities which she had held in check, could at last set out, bent, like his grandfather, Thutmose I, on adding conquest to conquest. Gathering his warriors together, he made up for all his years of chafing in forced retirement under Hatshepsut by marching up into Asia and taking city after city. He was the greatest conqueror of ancient Egypt and it was he who extended the Egyptian Empire to its farthest limits.

But the fighting spirit of the Eighteenth Dynasty was not to be expressed in battles and conquests only, for at last there was born of this powerful line Amenhotep IV, better known as Akhnaton, and this young man was to do his fighting in the realm of mind and spirit, he was to fight against war with the same dogged, stubborn courage his forebears had shown in battle. In his childhood, with Egypt going the way of war and bloodshed, Amon, the god of war, had become the most important god in the land. It was to the altar of Amon that men brought their offerings, so his priesthood had grown very rich and powerful. But the boy and his mother, Queen Tiy, talking often and thoughtfully together, knew that Amon gave death, not life, and they pondered long on the subject of God. Finally they came to this con-clusion—there was *one* God, *only* one, and that God was the giver of life, a power unseen, tender, intelligent, loving. He was one of whom no pictures, no statues, could be made because He was Life itself, the life that all living beings expressed in action, intelligence, love. This conception of God they called Aton or Lord and they knew no outward sign by which to represent Him save by the disk of the sun with many long arms radiating, like sunbeams, from it and ending in open hands as if giving life to the world.

When the young lad's father died and he became Pharaoh, he set out with all a youth's rashness and burning enthusiasm to establish his new religion. He would set free the thoughts of men from their fearful, dark superstitions. He would show them a God of sunshine, of gentleness and love, who asked only that men should live together in peace. Accordingly, he announced that Aton was the one and only God and that he would no longer bear the name of Amenhotep, which honored the war-god, Amon, but would henceforth be called Akhnaton, signifying, "The Glory of Aton." And in his youthful ignorance, he believed that people would heed him readily and take his truth to their hearts. But the priests of Amon were thunderstruck by his announcement. To preach a God of love and peace instead of a god of war— that threatened their power and prestige. Both openly and secretly they started to fight Akhnaton everywhere. Moreover, he soon discovered that it is not so simple a thing to make over the minds of men, for the mass of the people change their minds only very slowly. To give up their god of war, who had made them so powerful a nation, to give up all their other gods who seemed so real to their fancies, to accept in place of them a God who did not seem real because they could make no pictures or statues of Him— who could understand such a thing?

For years the young Pharaoh struggled with all the force and energy in him against the priests of Amon and the blindness of his people. War! They would all have war! At last, he left the capital, Thebes, to the priests of Amon and founded for himself and his followers the city of Akhetaton at the modern El-Amarna. But while he dreamed there his glorious dream of world peace, while he put forth all his efforts to achieve it, barbarian tribes began swarming down on the Empire and letters came pouring in to him from all his commanders in Asia, begging for aid in this crisis. But he still clung faithfully to his dream, he still refused to send more warriors into Asia. So, one by one, the cities of Asia were reconquered by Asiatics and the Empire of Egypt fell to pieces, while the men who could even remotely understand the young Pharaoh grew fewer and fewer in number and he was left ever more deserted. Finally, at the age of thirty, Akhnaton, brokenhearted, turned his face to the wall and died.

At his death he left seven young daughters but no sons and while two of these little girls were still playing with their dolls he had married them to boy princes whom he was training in the beloved truths of Aton. But his eldest son-in-law, who succeeded him, survived him by a year only, then the throne fell to Tut-ankh-amen, the childish husband of his second daughter. Being only a boy, Tut-ankh-amen soon fell under the power of the priests of Amon, who forced him to leave Akhnaton's city of Akhetaton and return with them to Thebes. When he died at the age of eighteen, he had done nothing save help wipe out all memory of Akhnaton and his great dream.

Never would history have remembered this youth save that his tomb was discovered in 1922 and, unlike most of the royal tombs, it had never been rifled by thieves, so it revealed more rich and beautiful objects than that of any other Pharaoh. There were chariots encased with platings of gold, couches bedecked with gold, golden mummy cases, pendants, collars, breast-plates, vases, caskets, statues, all most exquisitely wrought. And among these splendid things were found the little chair he had used as a child, his infant hood and tippet and one small glove, pathetically reminding anyone who sees the exhibits from his tomb in the Cairo Museum how young he was when he died since he still so treasured these keepsakes from his childhood that they were buried with him.

WITH TUT-ANKH-AMEN the magnificent Eighteenth Dynasty ended and it was the business of the Nineteenth Dynasty to try to reconquer Egypt's lost empire. Ramses II, called Ramses the Great, the most aggressive warrior of this line, conquered chief after chief in Africa and Asia, and it was under him that the twelve tribes of Israel, who had then lived for centuires in Egypt, were turned into slaves and brutally driven with whips to build his great new treasure cities. Yet with all his efforts and all his boastings on monuments, Ramses the Great never extended the empire to the limits of Thutmose III.

After him began the decline that goes with too much expansion, too much luxury and ease. Ever weaker grew the Pharaohs and their people, ever more disunited, until they gradually lost their prestige and all their possessions in Asia. To illustrate this period I have included the sorry story of Wenamon, who was sent on a mission into Syria during this age of decline. Poor old grumbling Wenamon, weak, inept and so muddle-headed he even forgot to take his letters of introduction with him! Able only to wail when he could not make the Syrian skipper of his vessel return to port to get his letters, wailing throughout his voyage when no Asiatic would pay any heed to his demands or his complaints—Wenamon symbolized the Egypt of this age just as the strong and adventurous Harkhuf symbolized her young strength.

Only once after this did Egypt really hold up her head and become again a great nation. That was under Pharaoh Psamtik in the seventh century B. C. But Psamtik's son Necho dreamed again of regaining Egypt's lost empire in Asia and that dream of empire was always her undoing. In the Bible times of the prophet Jeremiah, Pharaoh Necho, ambitiously pursuing this aim, was hopelessly defeated by that newly risen Asiatic war-lord, Nebuchadnezzar of Babylon. Thenceforth Egypt stayed at home. She was subject in time to the Persians, to the Greek line of the Ptolemies, and to Rome, but her own individual glory was forever lost. And at last she was to be swallowed up by Moslem Arab conquerors, so her people became the Moslem Egyptians we know in our world today.

TO SUM UP Egypt's contribution to history, it was here that people first grew out of the Stone Age into the age of metal. It was here that writing was invented and recorded history began. It was in Egypt that men invented the calendar and the shadow clock and discovered how to irrigate arid farm lands. It was Egyptians who were the first adventurers and explorers, the first great architects, artists, sculptors and craftsmen. They were the first great nation to work out a system of government and to learn by experience what happens when a nation sets out to conquer other nations and force its will upon them.

INDEX

INDEX

KEY TO PRONUNCIATION

ā as in māte   ä as in färm   ĭ as in ĭt   ū as in mūte
ă as in căt   ē as in ēve   ō as in mōte   ŭ as in cŭt
â as in câre   ĕ as in lĕt   ŏ as in nŏt   ōō as in fōōd
á as in ásk   ī as in mīnd   ô as in nôr   ŏŏ as in fŏŏt

261